Hidden Walks
in the Bay Area

HIDDEN WALKS

in the

BAY AREA

Pathways, Essays, and Yesterdays

By

Stephen Altschuler

Foreword by

Jacomena Maybeck

Western Tanager Press
Santa Cruz

Copyright © 1990 by Stephen Altschuler

Cover design by Lynn Piquett
Text design by Michael S. Gant
All photographs by the author unless otherwise credited
Maps by Andy Huber
Typography by TypaGraphix

All rights reserved. No portion of this book may be reproduced without permission in writing, except for quotations in critical articles or reviews.

ISBN: 0-934136-43-2

Library of Congress Card Catalog Number: 90-70115

Printed in the United States on 80 percent recycled paper

Western Tanager Press
1111 Pacific Avenue
Santa Cruz, CA 95060

This book is dedicated to those who love to walk, slow down, and reflect on things inside and out.

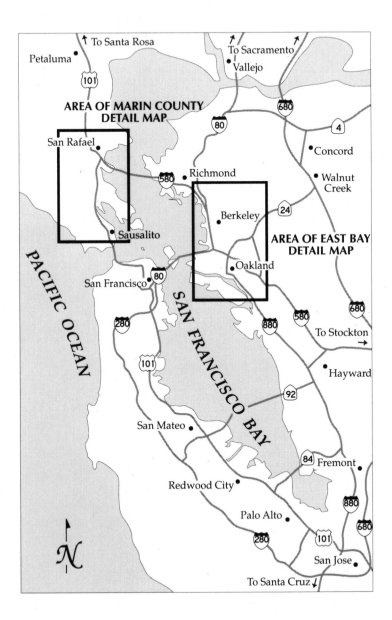

To Santa Rosa

Petaluma

101

To Sacramento

Vallejo

680

AREA OF MARIN COUNTY
DETAIL MAP

80

4

Concord

San Rafael

580 Richmond

Walnut
Creek

Berkeley

24

AREA OF EAST BAY
DETAIL MAP

Sausalito

Oakland

680

80

San Francisco

PACIFIC OCEAN

SAN FRANCISCO BAY

280

580

880

To Stockton

101

Hayward

92

San Mateo

84 Fremont

Redwood City

880

Palo Alto

680

280

101

San Jose

To Santa Cruz

N

Table of Contents

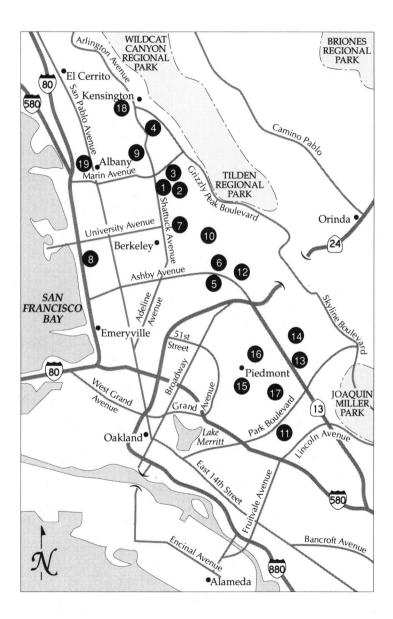

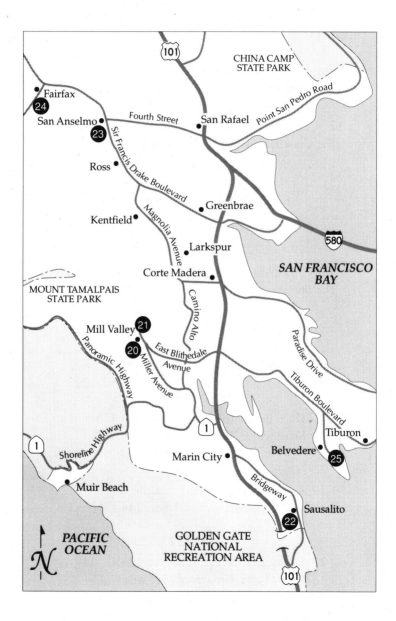

Acknowledgements

A book of this kind can be the brainchild of one person, but to bring it to completion and publication requires the energy of many. First, I'd like to thank my publisher Hal Morris, editor-in-chief Lauren Wickizer, and copy editor and book designer Michael Gant for their encouragement, faith, and expertise during this project. They are real professionals and it was/is a pleasure working with them. Thanks, too, to cartographer Andy Huber, a recent UC Berkeley graduate, who managed to perform his Macintosh wonders while working another full-time job; to David Rains Wallace, who read some of the essays when the concept of a book was just a seed, and whose comments helped the seed grow; and to those who provided firsthand historical and cartographic information — people such Bertha Underhill, Jacomena Maybeck, the Guyots of the present-day Hillside Club, the staffs of the Berkeley Historical Society, the Berkeley Architectural Heritage Association, the Mill Valley Public Library, the Kensington Public Library, the Claremont Hotel, Fairfax Parks and Recreation, and the chambers of commerce and public works departments of almost every town and city covered in this book. The job of town engineer may be a prosaic one, but those people know their hidden paths and rights-of-way.

Also much gratitude goes to those who provided the emotional, social, spiritual, and, sometimes, logistical support so needed by a free-lance writer taking on his first book project: Orion, Gloria St. John, Benjamin Tasner, Bob Bartel, Morgan Alwell, Bernice Moore, Terry Ojure, Gregg Levoy, Robin Sierra, Sarah Greenberg, Jon Larson, Wiebke Larson, Brent Ryder, Mason Drukman, Pat Tribble, Zeida Rothman, Lila (a most loving and faithful cat), and Jean Maxwell, who, when she reaches 100 in the year 2000 (Jean, your goal is now in print, so I'll be holding you to it!), will still, I'm sure, be strolling by, listening to, and composing poems about Strawberry Creek in mind and/or body.

Finally, special thanks go to my parents — Mo, who, if he were still alive, would have propped up a copy of this book on his nightstand and looked at it every night, and Rose, who has given me continuous love, understanding, and encouragement.

Foreword

This is a book for people with a little time. Time to explore, to wander in new places, to see a part of your town you never knew.

Did you know that there was a network of paths and walkways all through the Berkeley hills and in Marin County and Albany? This is a guide book and I can hardly wait to copy out a set of directions and go.

The Bernard Maybeck family liked paths — shortcuts for school kids. They gave ten-foot strips of their land so agile people could cut between lots and streets. When I was young and married to Wallen Maybeck, I walked down Buena Vista Way to Hawthorne Steps, on to Euclid Avenue and veered left to the Vine Lane steps that led straight down to Shattuck Avenue and my marketing. Wallen took this route for years on his way to his San Francisco office. People set their watches by him!

This network of walks is as fabulous as the sewers of Paris, only cleaner and fresher. It is an inner world. It is full of bits of history as well as peace and calm.

You become a more intimate citizen of your town by exploring its neighborhoods on foot. You get to see new views of it — see houses you never knew existed and native plants you'd forgotten about. In fact, you get enriched.

You even find waterfalls and creeks. In Berkeley? Most are buried under streets, but on these walks you meet some face to face. Hear the gurgle. See the ripple. There is so much that goes with creeks; you owe it to yourself to explore them.

When we built our home in Kensington our children would never have found the school without paths and trails. We grown-ups should not do without trails in our lives either.

JACOMENA MAYBECK
Berkeley, California
December 6, 1989

Introduction

I discovered — really started — walking while living in New Hampshire a number of years ago, when my car was vandalized one snowy Christmas Eve. Instead of fixing it or buying another, I chose to see the incident as a metaphysical message to go on foot and skis for almost two years. Walking became more than my favorite pastime. It was how I got around.

I began to see and appreciate things that had been only a blur before. The pace of life slowed. I heard birds, smelled flowers, petted cats, fended off dogs, talked to neighbors, admired houses, listened to creeks, and sat by lakes. I could hear myself think, and so did more of it — that clear thinking that comes from a quieter mind. I could define and examine what I was feeling since the events of the day could age in my mind before the next day's events began. Walking allowed me perspective.

I eventually rejoined the world of the wheeled, came to California — *the* world of the wheeled — and settled in the Bay Area. Fortunately, I also kept my love of walking and soon found a network of lanes, paths, and steps, relatively hidden in the residential hills, inviting me to thread my way throughout and around. These pathways, along with trails in less developed areas, made the Bay Area a walker's paradise.

The following walks and thoughts will open up a Bay Area you may not know. It is an area of waterfalls and creeks and parks and trees and muddy paths and birds and distinctive houses and midday quiet and hidden places within its towns and cities, far removed from the bustle of Telegraph and Bancroft or Shattuck and Center or Fourteenth and Broadway or Route 101. This is a more personal Bay Area, where you can become intimate with its natural history, architecture, and nature.

All the walks described are accessible by public transportation, at all times of year, and are appropriate for most ages and physical conditions. Some take the walker quite close to homes, so I urge you to be sensitive to residents' needs for privacy and quiet. The pathways, for the most part, were laid out in the early twentieth century when large hillside tracts were subdivided and neighborhoods and towns developed. It was a time when streets were used more for walking than driving, when people needed an efficient way of getting to a neighbor's door or down to the Key (transportation) System to get to work. The recreational use I'm suggesting here must carry with it the spirit of that peaceful era.

The paths are generally not wheelchair-accessible, although there are some which are paved throughout (most are probably too steep for wheelchairs, but adventurous people might try some). Most of the parks mentioned *are* accessible to the disabled, however. The routes can be easily modified for distance and direction to accommodate different degrees of fitness, time, weather, and mood. They are a starting-point, really, for you may find paths and lanes yet undiscovered, and perhaps some not mentioned in this book. (There are 91 public pathways in Berkeley alone.)

When I discovered the hidden Keeler Path on the "High Parks and a Primitive Path" walk in Berkeley, for example, I felt like Drake or Muir or Lewis and Clark. This magical path was omitted from local maps. I had charted an uncharted path of the West!

I hope you enjoy these walks as much as I do. They offer a safe, convenient, fun way to taste nature (with their creeks, waterfalls, and plant life), get good exercise (stairways provide one of the best aerobic exercises around), and appreciate local history (which comes alive when you see examples of it first hand). Make each outing an adventure, using public transportation or foot power, if possible, and on the way home, talking or thinking about everything you remember seeing, hearing, smelling, and learning.

I hope, too, you are stimulated to further thought and reflection by the short histories, essays, and architectural and botanical references. To walk and muse is an old tradition honed by Thoreau, Muir, Leopold, Murie, and Dillard. To do so as you explore these pathways will help insure they will remain part of the Bay Area's heritage. May they bring you and your family not only closer to the towns and cities of this great region, but closer to yourself and each other.

Good walking!

Berkeley

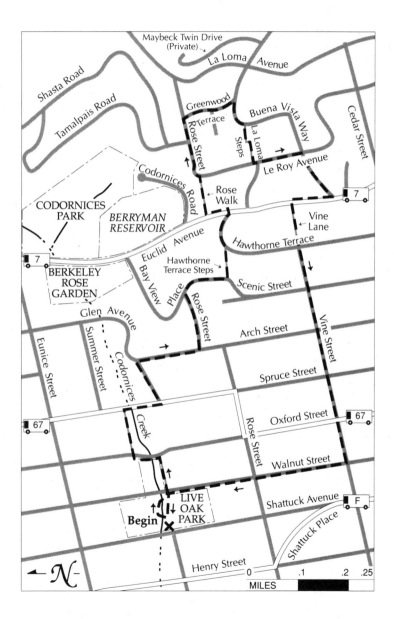

1

The Live Oak & Rose Walk

Terrain: *easy to moderate; improved lanes and steps*
Bus Line: *F*
Parks: *Codornices (on Euclid near Eunice), Live Oak (on Shattuck near Rose), Berkeley Rose Garden*
Shops: *Walnut Square shops, Shattuck and Vine*
Distance: *2.5 miles*
Directions: *Go north on Shattuck from University, past Rose to Live Oak Park on right.*

Slicing through the heart of North Berkeley, the Rose Walk offers a short interlude into a Berkeley of another time: pink concrete steps and pillars, tiered gardens, houses of stucco and redwood, red tiles, mission-style roofs, expansive bay views, and flowers in bloom year-round. Yet, in 1923, the area covered in this walk had been completely gutted by fire. It was rebuilt under the architectural guidance of the Hillside Club (see page 38) and its favorite architect, Bernard Maybeck, who helped restore the area with simplicity, grace, and more fire-resistant building materials. With Live Oak Park, this walk combines naturalness and elegance that can help calm a busy midday mind or get your family's weekend off to a good start.

The Rose Walk got its name from Rose Avenue, an early street, and was designed and built by Bernard Maybeck in 1913, and paid for by Hillside Club residents of the neighborhood. The elfin cottages adjacent to the Rose Walk were designed by Henry Gutterson shortly after the fire in 1923, all with art, nature, and simplicity in mind. In 1976, the Rose Walk was given landmark status.

This jaunt begins on a quiet part of Shattuck Avenue past Rose Street, at Live Oak Park, a 5.5-expanse of oaks, redwoods, lawns, sporting facilities, a rambling section of Codornices Creek, picnic areas, and a community theater. Live Oak Park is one of Berkeley's oldest, developed in 1914, and is also the most heavily used park in town. About half a million people enjoy its indoor and outdoor facilities each year.

Start in front of the Live Oak Theater, opposite Berryman Street, noticing the beautifully crafted wooden sign for the park, and walk toward the greenwood of live oaks and redwoods down to the sturdy wood bridge crossing meandering Codornices Creek. Turn right just over the bridge, along the path that follows the creek, to another bridge, this time a finely crafted stone structure. Cross the bridge then take the path immediately to the left, still along the creek, going through the tunnel that passes under Walnut Street. (You can also take the path that leads up and across Walnut. It's less hidden but probably safer.)

You're now on the grounds of the Berkeley Art Center, a gift to the city by the Rotary Club and an interesting gallery open noon to 5 P.M., Thursday through Sunday. Continue past the center, keeping the creek on your left, and go up the steps straight ahead to Oxford Street. Go left to the next crosswalk, cross, and find the Berryman Path, marked with a sign, at this point. It's next to the spacious grounds of the East Bay Chinese Alliance Church.

The short but verdant path leads to Spruce Street, where you turn right. Opposite the church, go left on Glen Avenue, admiring the huge brown-shingled, First Bay Tradition house at #2204. Take a right onto Arch Street, where you can see the First Bay Tradition styles of architect Julia Morgan at #1320 and #1324,

built in 1906 and 1910 respectively, and her mentor, Bernard Maybeck, at #1325, built in 1906.

Go left at Rose, walking up to Scenic Avenue and bearing right. The old Needham Apartment building at #1358, with its redwood exterior, was obviously influenced by First Bay architects. Listen to the birds inside the indoor aviary next to #1360, with its small, screened outdoor perch.

Continue past plum and pepper trees to the Hawthorne Steps, marked on the left, and ascend gracefully past toyon, privet, and cedar, emerging onto Hawthorne Terrace, where a left turn reveals a different Maybeck at #1408. The large brown-shingle at #1404, with its leaded-glass windows and gracious laurel tree, was designed by Julia Morgan.

The short street joins busy Euclid, which you'll need to cross before heading north (left) to find the Rose Walk immediately to your right. (A little farther on Euclid is the Berkeley Rose Garden and Codornices Park.) The pink concrete steps and pillars (Maybeck preferred the soft pink color to white concrete), lead up and almost out of time past roses, antique lampposts, stone benches, and gingerbread redwood cottages, coming out onto, again, Rose Street. Bear left on Rose, observing John Galen Howard's large brown-shingled house across the street at #1401 Le Roy, up to Greenwood Terrace, where you turn right as the grade now levels.

If I could pick a street in Berkeley to live out my days in peace and solitude it would be Greenwood Terrace. The huge Monterey pines there are among the tallest in the state and are more than 100 years old. Originally the area was owned by a Captain Thomas, who planted the pine forest, along with orchards and grain fields, all surrounding his home overlooking the bay. For years, the area was called La Loma Park until it was subdivided. To your right, notice the lawns of Greenwood Common, a group of modern private residences, and to your left an assortment of interesting and attractive houses and cottages, including a

Maybeck at #1476 (though not one of his more interesting designs) and John Galen Howard houses at #1459 (set far back from the road and not particularly visible) and #1486 with its long redwood shingles, decorative sun porch, and red brick sidewalk — all of which survived the 1923 fire.

At the end of Greenwood Terrace, you have a choice. To the left on Buena Vista Way and up past La Loma Avenue takes you deeper into Bernard Maybeck country and some prime originals of his, both before and after the fire. This is not essentially an architectural tour and the walking is fairly hazardous due to traffic, so I've chosen not to include this in this walk, but I'll mention some of the houses in case you go that way. If you choose not to see the Maybeck houses, just skip the rest of this long paragraph. At #2704 Buena Vista, at the corner of La Loma, Maybeck built this home in 1915, using a fire-resistant roof, which allowed it to survive the fire. Maybeck's own house, which was perhaps the finest example of his ideals, was located just across the street on Buena Vista and was completely destroyed. Down La Loma at #1515, Maybeck used a Mediterranean style with arches, round windows, and wood trellises, reminiscent of a Pompeian villa, building a house that was not only fire-resistant but also earthquake-proof, using reinforced concrete. The owner had been a professor of geology. Back up to Buena Vista, is the pink "Bubblestone Studio" at #2711, flanked by eucalyptus and ginkgo. Maybeck designed the house in 1924 after the fire, attaching burlap bags saturated with a lightweight concrete called Bubblestone over the wood frame with wire. When the unusual shingles dried, he had a fire-resistant exterior. Continuing up the street to the left marked Maybeck Twin Drive (this is still Buena Vista as Maybeck Twin Drive actually starts farther up and is private) are Maybeck homes at #2733, with its Swiss chalet-like garage door, and one he designed for his son, Wallen, and daughter-in-law, Jacomena at #2751. The last house of interest on this mini-tour is at #2800, partially seen through the toyon where the street bends to the left. Not a Maybeck design, it was built by his good friends, the Boyntons, who called it the Temple of Wings, the inspiration of Mrs. Boynton, who dreamed of living in a Greek temple. It got through the fire with its 34 Corinthian columns intact and facing majestically toward the bay. The Boyntons were close friends with the famous dancer Isadora Duncan and often threw parties featuring Greek dancing and their favorite, and some say only, food: nuts and dried fruit. It was either the food or their reputed eccentricity that caused locals to call this neighborhood "Nut Hill."

Now back to "The Live Oak and Rose Walk." Bear right onto Buena Vista Way, at the end of Greenwood Terrace, where you'll quickly see a metal sign post without a sign, an aging redwood fence with bamboo panels, and pink concrete pillars (indicating Maybeck's influence), supporting a Japanese-style archway, all to the left of #2597. The red brick steps beside all this are the La Loma Steps, an old, well-constructed shortcut that zigzags past pink concrete pillars and under wooden trellises on its wending way down to Le Roy Avenue and a trellised gateway. Go left on Le Roy, then take an immediate right onto Buena Vista, admiring the delicate arrangement of Japanese maples in front of #2525, before coming to Euclid.

At the corner is another unique Maybeck original. It's at #1537 Euclid and was built for a music teacher in 1914 and rebuilt with a fireproof tile roof after the 1923 fire. The stucco house with the tawny trim, a bridged passageway, and balconies Maybeck liked so much combines several styles. The elegant tree growing on the ledge beneath the long arched window on Euclid is the cajuput, a native of Indonesia. It's still a place of music, now called the Maybeck Recital Hall, with Sunday concerts open to the public. (Call 415/848-3228 for a brochure.)

A short way north (right) on Euclid see the signpost for Vine Lane and Euclid. The black scrolled wrought iron archway spelling out the name of this lane is the most ornate and obvious entrance to a Berkeley lane. Many signposts marking pathways throughout the Bay Area are missing, but this one has survived the most covetous of minds.

Descend Vine Lane past live oak, rhododendron, camellia, and loquat to Hawthorne Terrace with Vine Street straight ahead. Stay on Vine, passing an array of interesting houses and landscape designs, including the white fence, brick wall, and arched wood gate at Scenic; the Tudor Revival at #2333 that looks like it could have been shipped whole from England; the striking Congregation Beth El synagogue at Arch, with its tree of life front door, stained-glass windows, and row of olive trees; the winsome grouping of birch trees at #2289; the red-shingled, green-trimmed house at #2277, which was remodeled from an 1898 barn; the turreted and towering Victorian painted lady at #2213; the three more Victorians just past Oxford; and the First Bay Tradition Friends Meeting House at the northeast corner of Walnut and Vine.

Turn right onto Walnut, past the mission-style Berkeley-Richmond Jewish Community Center, a building with city and federal landmark status, built in 1915, that is the only public building in Berkeley designed by Ernest Coxhead, the noted architect who designed many early houses in the area. It was originally a school building and features arched walkways and courtyards.

Cross Rose, soon reentering Live Oak Park on the left. Take the path to the left of the creek, sharing it with squirrels, jays, and an occasional homeless street person, out to Shattuck. It's the last chance to applaud Codornices Creek before it disappears under downtown Berkeley.

If you still have some energy, feast on three classic, pre–1923 fire Maybeck originals at #1210 and #1208, both set back from the street, and #1200, closer to the street but partially hidden by a huge Bishop pine and a wooden trellis in front. To me, his houses and landscape designs seem like the work of a man who enjoyed life.

Bernard Maybeck & Architecture

When North Berkeley burnt to the ground in 1923, the man who was in demand to redesign its homes was the same one who had designed most of the area originally: Bernard Ralph Maybeck. The son of a German woodcarver, Maybeck had apprenticed as a furniture maker in New York before going to France to study at the leading architectural school of the time, the Ecole des Beaux Arts in Paris. Here, Maybeck learned about expressing the character of a building through exposing the interior and exterior structure rather than covering it with paneling, wallpaper, or paint, as was the common practice. He developed, too, from helping to plan one of France's largest public gardens, a sense of landscape design and the blending of a building with its environment.

When he came to California in 1889, Maybeck was ready to apply his ideas practically. "Stone and wood construction proper bears the same relation to architecture that the piano, for instance, does to the music played upon it," he wrote. "Music and architecture are vehicles of expression for phases of our human experience." He was in the right place at the right time since the California Arts and Crafts Movement, which advocated a return to aesthetic simplicity in one's life, was at the height of its popularity. He began discussing his ideas with Charles Keeler, a Berkeley poet and architectural critic who wrote one of the bibles of the movement, *The Simple Home.*

In 1894, Maybeck designed Keeler's Berkeley home, manifesting all his principles in such features as an unpainted redwood exterior that matched the house in color and mood with the surrounding land, exposed interior infrastructure, and even built-in furniture, using dovetail and wooden-peg joinery both functionally and decoratively. The house served as a model for subsequent houses in North Berkeley and was a vanguard for the First Bay Tradition of architecture that spread to many

Bernard Ralph Maybeck (with saw) helping design and construct the clubhouse (no longer there) at Codornices Park in 1915. (PHOTO COURTESY OF BERKELEY HISTORICAL SOCIETY)

other parts of the Bay Area. Though modified in external appearance, the Keeler house still stands at 1770 Highland Place.

Maybeck went on to design the Palace of Fine Arts for the 1915 Panama Pacific Exposition in San Francisco, showing his Beaux Arts versatility beyond the brown-shingled single home. He was a man of deep feeling, as these following words of his on architectural design show:

> We must use those forms in architecture and gardening that will affect the emotions in such a way as to produce in the individual the same modified sadness as the galleries do. This process is similar to that of matching the color of ribbons. You pick up a blue ribbon, hold it alongside the sample in your hand, and at a glance you know it matches or it does not.

You do the same with architecture: you examine a historic form and see whether the effect it produced on your mind matches the feeling you are trying to portray — a modified sadness or a sentiment in a minor key.

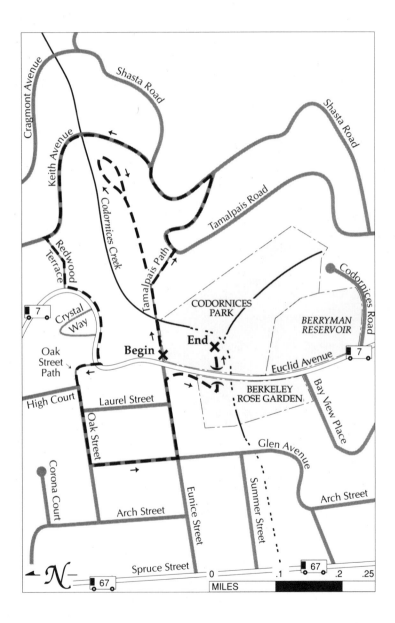

CRAGMONT AVENUE

Shasta Road

Shasta Road

Keith Avenue

Codornices Creek

Tamalpais Road

Tamalpais Path

Codornices Road

Redwood Terrace

Crystal Way

7

CODORNICES PARK

BERRYMAN RESERVOIR

Oak Street Path

Begin

End

Euclid Avenue

7

High Court

Laurel Street

BERKELEY ROSE GARDEN

Bay View Place

Oak Street

Glen Avenue

Corona Court

Arch Street

Eunice Street

Summer Street

Arch Street

N

Spruce Street

67

0   .1   .2   .25

MILES

67

2
The Way of Waterfalls

Terrain: *easy to steep; improved lanes and steps; unimproved trails*
Bus Line: 7
Parks: *Codornices, Berkeley Rose Garden, Tilden Regional and Wildcat Regional*
Shops: *Walnut Square near Shattuck and Vine*
Distance: *2 miles*
Directions: *From University Avenue, turn left on Shattuck to Cedar. Go right to Euclid, then left to Codornices Park/Rose Garden.*

No less than 14 creeks flow through Berkeley, most starting in the hills, and trickling down through deep gorges, hidden gullies and culverts. It is rare to see a creek as the land flattens. They'll probably soon be listed with the San Joaquin kit fox as an endangered species. But on this walk, you will see some of Berkeley's more wild and scenic creeks as well as a couple of gorgeous waterfalls. Addenda to the walk may be needed in years to come, since the East Bay hills are still growing, and, along with continual earthquake activity, pushing new sources of water out from underground. Even in severe drought years, many of Berkeley's creeks are fed by these underground springs and continue to run year-round.

Take the paved path at the north end of Codornices Park, at Euclid Avenue and Eunice Street, across from the Berkeley Rose Garden, and descend west toward a grove of redwoods and bay

laurel. Cross a wooden bridge over the North Fork of Codornices Creek and a couple of small waterfalls. Water sounds begin
to muffle the traffic noise here. Bird song becomes more aud-
ible, harmonizing with children's laughter in the park. Laurel
abounds. Ascend a spiraling concrete stairway which is the start
of the Tamalpais Path. Like its namesake mountain to the west,
this path of 188 steps climbs steeply. But before you consider
turning back, take just 64 steps, the easy first third, stop and
look to your left.

You'll see a small dirt path, unmarked, that winds through
a grove of redwoods and continues along the ridge above lush
Benner's Canyon. Forget-me-nots, irises, ivy, and clover blanket
the canyon at different times of year. As you continue to walk,
the sound of falling water intensifies. Ahead are the falls — yes,
the falls — dropping several levels. If you have time, it's a wonderful place to stop, look, listen, meditate — anything quiet. A resident hummingbird can sometimes be seen sipping from the
falls, and the sound of the water can transport you to a high
mountain gorge in your mind.

Above and to the right take the wooden walkway and keep
bearing to the right. Return to the Tamalpais Path via the same
canyon ridge path.

Continue ascending the remaining 124 steps. To help motivate
you, I should add here that another waterfall lies ahead and that
the climb is good for your heart and at least it's not snowing
and . . . there, it's over.

To the left on Tamalpais Road, admire #149, built in 1914,
with its stone walls and wooden gates, its odd long shingles and
broad beams over and under small bay windows. There are also
turrets, flagpoles, split-rail fences and — the maestro of the
orchestra — a sprawling interior live oak.

Swing around the bend on Tamalpais Road past houses rang-
ing in style from Gothic to Tudor to First Bay Tradition to
Redwood Empire to Snow White and the Seven Dwarfs to

modern. It's all there. There are also huge Australian tree ferns and more live oaks before you reach Shasta Road. About a hundred years ago, there was a dairy farm with grazing cows on this corner. Turn left and continue to the first intersection.

This is the start of Keith Avenue (named for the turn-of-the-century Berkeley landscape painter William Keith), which, after a few hundred feet, leads to that other promised waterfall. Water from the Keith Falls, which is part of Codornices Creek, drops four levels before disappearing through the culvert, under the street, and on to the previously described waterfall below.

Continue on Keith to the Redwood Terrace Path on your left, just past #1140. The path is unmarked so watch for it closely. Then descend 131 steps, feasting on bay views, mini-meadows, colorful gardens, and, finally, Euclid Avenue.

Go left on Euclid and cross the street quickly at the Oak Street Path (careful! there's no crosswalk). Follow the Oak Street Path — there's only one oak, the remaining trees being laurel — up a few red stone steps. Exit onto High Court and go left past Laurel Street. Straight ahead, follow a dirt road which leads to a dirt path to the left, both unmarked and unnamed. You're on the right path if you see a large, shapely palm ahead of you. Being a native Easterner, I'm continually surprised by palms. They remind me of all the winters I no longer need to endure but can actually live through comfortably. This one is the hardy California Palm or Desert Fan, the only palm native to California out of 4,000 species worldwide.

At the end of this path is the junction of Oak Street and Glen Avenue. Go left on Glen, then left on Eunice Street for the short ascent to Euclid. For the grand conclusion, take the steps at the southwest corner of Euclid and Eunice down to the funhouse foot tunnel (sharp left at bottom of steps) that passes under Euclid, shooting you through to Codornices Park. This 10.6-acre park used to be a steep, rocky gulch, overgrown with brush and inhabited by many quail (*codornices* is Spanish for quail). But during the early years of the Depression, the Works Progress Administration (WPA) helped develop it and the terraced paths of the Berkeley Rose Garden into showcases. Today you'll find swings, slides, picnic tables, lawns, an open and natural section of Codornices Creek, wildflowers, trails, many species of roses, summer wedding ceremonies, views of San Francisco Bay, tennis courts, drinking fountains, and . . . rest rooms. You couldn't ask for more.

Creek Walking

C reeks are the heart-blood of a town — arteries that descend from the hills, greeting developed areas with that absolute trust that is common in the natural world. And how a community returns the greeting is a measure of its spirit. Does it slam its doors with culverts, embalming the creek beneath concrete and asphalt? Does it bully it into back alleys where it becomes little more than a cesspool? Or does it showcase the creek, garnishing its banks with trees and flowers, embracing it, and acknowledging the vital part it can play in people's lives?

Berkeley is fortunate to have several creeks still not fully encased by concrete. Capistrano, Codornices, Strawberry, Blackberry, Schoolhouse — the names are full of lightness and dance, full of whimsy and poetry.

A creek balances the nature of a town. A creek has nothing to do with commerce or higher education or political leanings. It doesn't try to better itself, for it has no self to better. It simply advances: faster in wet weather, slower in dry. A creek is a model of unity and simplicity, offering a frenetic town relief from its willful activities.

There's been talk of breaking up some of the downtown parking lots that entomb Strawberry Creek — of resurrecting it and restoring its rightful place. If the creek were to flow downtown with renewed grace and grandeur, as it does on the university campus, the soul of the town would be nourished. At one time, as recently as 200 years ago, this area was meadow and scattered woodland, filled with bunch grasses, clover, and coast live oak, its streams running into a much larger bay, its skies thick with migratory birds.

And, in deep ways, some of this natural beauty is still here. On the surface is a crust of concrete, but if left unmaintained, even for as little as a hundred years, it would all return to the softness of soil, sand, and silt. The streets would heave and crack, and plant life and water would seep in, acidifying and decomposing the rock. Look at any abandoned parking lot and see oxalis and wild mustard making ready a meadow.

Yes, we need to welcome the creeks back. We need reminders of our own naturalness. We need to see moving water with its places of stillness — places of quiet reflection within a form that constantly changes.

A human being, like a creek, is also moving, changing, flowing; yet we often fight against this nature, causing inner conflict and suffering. Even happiness becomes a fight, for its base is aversion to pain.

There is no fight to a creek's life. In winter it is full and fast. In summer it is a thin silver ribbon meandering along, letting gravity and the lowest places determine its course. A creek's life is not a problem to be solved nor a struggle to be overcome. There is no sense of unfolding or becoming. There is no tension, no frustration, no anxiety, no expecting. There is just the water-course way taking the path of least resistance in complete harmony with the earth-course way. The two are inseparable — earth and water. And it's that quality of harmony that makes creek walking so appealing and nurturing.

In the hills above Berkeley, there is a section of Wildcat Creek — a short stretch of wildness — that has within it the same spirit as the most awesome of any Sierra white water. Walking there is quieting. The imaginary line between "creek" and "self" is gone. There is just water and woods and no thought about them.

It is in that moment of quietness that love arises. It was always there, but the silence of mind allows it space to manifest. It is an extraordinary moment, deep and expansive, yet ephemeral. Thought returns, but all is now changed. The earth is more a real mother.

Below, water, unburdened by time, barrels through a gap in

some large rocks. Soon it will disappear somewhere on its run to the bay. But for now, in this place, it is a creek that awakens aliveness.

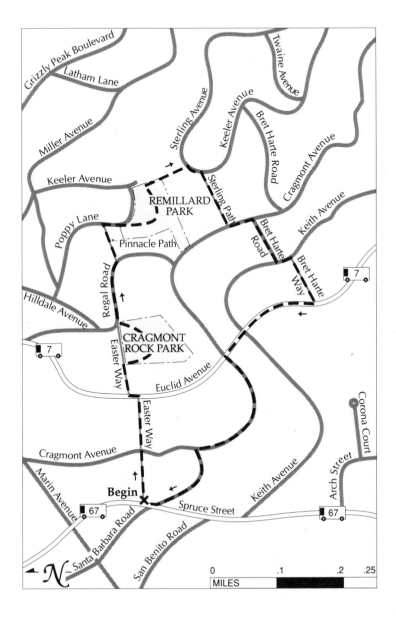

3

High Parks &
a Primitive Path

Terrain: *moderate; improved lanes and steps; unimproved trail*
Bus Line: *67*
Parks: *Cragmont Rock, Remillard, Live Oak on Shattuck near Rose*
Shops: *Walnut Square near Shattuck and Vine*
Distance: *1.7+ miles*
Directions: *Go north on Shattuck off University to Rose. Turn right to Spruce then left to just past Santa Barbara.*

The North Berkeley hills were once a favored vacation spot for San Franciscans who ferried across, seeking respite from the city's faster pace and denser summer fog. The vacation homes are now family homes, and the area has become one of Berkeley's most desirable, despite the fact that most of it is particularly vulnerable to earthquake activity on the Hayward Fault. The cracks in the concrete and asphalt paths mirror the cracks in surrounding foundations. Some houses are literally sliding down the hill.

You'll be safe on the paths and lanes, though, and this walk goes to the heart of some of North Berkeley's surprises. Prepare for expansive parks, unusual houses, and a primitive path in the middle of it all.

Start at Spruce Street just north of Santa Barbara Road, where on the east side of Spruce are concrete steps and a railing just before #933, the number marked on a pink concrete retaining wall. This is the start of "Easter Way." (There is a signpost here, but, as of this writing, no sign.) Ascend Easter Way, somewhat steeply, on mostly steps, past quiet gardens, a variety of wooden fences, gates, and entrance ways, crossing equally quiet Cragmont Avenue, noting the massive brown-shingled house to the left, still rising until a perfect Japanese maple bows before the steps leading onto busy Euclid Avenue. Cross carefully and, to the left, look for the continuation of Easter Way, to the right of #971, where there is currently a signpost but no sign.

From here, the lane continues to rise for a short way, past an ancient tree house in the brushy garden at #75 to the right, until it opens into Cragmont Rock Park. There, a large lawn greets you to your right, bordered by a tall deodar — a cedar tree native to India — along with pine and coast redwoods. At the top of the lawn, a dirt path to the right passes a fine stone-backed, tiled seat, looking out onto Point Richmond, the Bay, and Mt. Tamalpais — a good spot for sunset watching. But keep exploring: with three acres, this park has much to offer.

Continuing into the park via a paved utility driveway, is another lawn, on a plateau and suitable for sunbathing or short-distance Frisbee throwing. To the west is a open-sided shelter, with old stone pillars, posts, and beams, etched deeply with the initials of lovers and other immortals. Looking out from here, you're treated to great views of the bay, the Marin hills, San Francisco, and the Golden Gate Bridge. There are also views of the campus and the hills to the south and east, beyond the stone wall border. Of course, in rain and fog, forget the views and just enjoy being where no one else in Berkeley is at that moment.

In addition to its views, lawns, and shelter, don't miss the magical side trails down and around the park. They don't really go anywhere nor do most of them interconnect, but if the park is crowded, as it is on most warm, summer weekends, they offer some solitude, quiet, and a deeper taste of nature. An old stone building on the north side of the park is actually one of the more architecturally interesting rest rooms in the Bay Area. There are more paths near it as well, leading to a small but noble redwood grove.

When you're ready to move on, continue past the park, turn right on Regal Road and notice the regal hacienda, with the Spanish red-tile roof, a wrought iron gate, and a craftsman stone wall that ranks as one of Berkeley's finest. It's the kind of place I envision the original owner of the East Bay, Don Luis Maria Peralta, living in. Descend past the sprawling house to Pinnacle Path on the left, next to the pink stucco house at #979. Climb its privet-lined and lighted steps to Poppy Lane, with the distinctive modern craftsman house straight ahead, a welcome change from the surrounding stucco.

Turn right on Poppy to Remillard Park, where you'll find a four-acre, mostly quiet park with an open lawn and a huge hunk of volcanic rock, about 10 million years old, that is used by the Sierra Club and other climbing aficionados for challenging rock-climbing practice. Climbing is the only way to get to the top, which is 800 feet above sea level and inch for inch is as formidable as anything you'll find in the Sierras.

I say the park is *mostly* quiet because judging from the amount of broken glass on the side trails around the rock, I expect quite a bit of partying goes on during summer nights. I was hard pressed to find a safe place on the lower rocks to sit and eat my lunch, but I finally did find a snug spot beneath tall pines, bay laurels, and a surprise crab apple tree.

During the day, particularly weekdays, you'll find Remillard to be a peaceful park. But the best part of it may be the way out! Enter the nicely equipped playground, circle the sand box play area, climb a few wooden steps and proceed to your right to an earthen trail, fringed with blackberry vines, that leads into a wild-looking area.

This is one of North Berkeley's most primitive paths. When you're deep into it, let your mind settle and savor this place of no-time, of no-name. For the path actually has no official name.

Continue on this urban wilderness tour until a low laurel heralds the end, which looks like someone's backyard. Worry not. This is a public path, not listed on local maps but referred to as Keeler Path by some locals since it connects two separate sections of Keeler Avenue. It is also a path that Charles Keeler, the turn-of-the-century Berkeley poet and one of the prime movers behind the network of pedestrian paths in North Berkeley, would have (and may have) used and enjoyed.

Just past the shingled, multibalconied house on your left, exit onto Keeler, then bear right to the Sterling Path, marked by a sign on the garage of #1072. Descend, under oak and pine, past ground-level stone cairns and a giant century plant, traversing concrete and earth, and ending with improved steps down to Cragmont Avenue.

Go left on Cragmont, then take an immediate right onto Bret Harte Road (Bret Harte, the writer of western novels and stories lived and worked in Oakland), down to Keith Avenue. Just to your left here see the sign Bret Harte Way, to the left of #1100, a path with Japanese fences, a street light, an inviting wooden seat, an assortment of ornamental plants, and out-of-plumb steps that have marched to a different drummer over the years. At the bottom is Euclid.

Go right on Euclid, past Keith, then turn left on Cragmont, a gentle, winding Hillside Club of a street with bay views and a pleasing mix of brown-shingle and stucco bungalows bordered by brick walls and Bishop pines. This leads to equally picturesque Santa Barbara Road, where you turn left, safely returning from high Berkeley parks and a wild path.

The Berkeley Fire of 1923

O n September 17, 1923, a terrible grass and brush fire, originating in Wildcat Canyon and fanned by strong, hot northeast winds, swept over North Berkeley, blowing flaming leaves, grass, and roof shingles onto other houses as far as one and a half miles away. Tentacles of fire raced down through the hills toward the downtown area. Codornices Canyon was a wind tunnel, as "many of the smaller homes and garages were wiped off as if by magic," wrote fire chief G. Sydney Rose in his report.

It started at noon, and when it was over that night, almost 700 houses and buildings, including homes, apartments, fraternities and sororities, a firehouse, and a church were destroyed or damaged, and 4,000 people were homeless. Were it not for the winds shifting back toward the hills, the fire would have consumed the downtown area and quickly spread to Oakland.

So swift did it move, that residents seemed dazed as they sacked their own houses, roofs ablaze, to save whatever they could. One eyewitness saw such a resident falter along the street holding the only possession she could salvage: a telephone book.

The fire rivaled the 1906 San Francisco earthquake blaze in intensity, and, as then, the community responded to the call for help. The chancellor of UC Berkeley canceled classes, as the Campanile bell rang out the alarm. Some 4,000 students and faculty reportedly answered the call for volunteers, and the administration joined with the Red Cross in establishing refugee care centers on campus. Although busy fighting their own fires in the hot, muggy weather, fire companies from Oakland, Richmond, Piedmont, and Emeryville sped to the scene. A contingent of 200 firefighters from San Francisco ferried across the bay and helped save the downtown area. And even San Jose was en route when the winds suddenly reversed. In all, 2,000 firefighters eventually arrived. Fortunately no one died, but property losses were estimated at $10 million.

As today, one of the problems was water: there was a scarcity due partly to poor management of resources and little public consciousness around conservation. Also, the water mains and pipes were too small, limiting the volume and pressure needed to fight fires. As a result, some buildings were dynamited in a desperate attempt to bring the fire closer to ground level. For several years, North Berkeley looked like a war zone, with only brick chimneys standing as stark monuments.

It was a devastating blow to the residents, particularly Hillside Club members, who had labored so hard to beautify the area. But by then, the club's influence was well intact, and the rebuilding proceeded according their recommendations. They were even successful in blocking an attempt to ban construction with wood shingles, helping defeat the measure in a referendum. The vote reversed a city ordinance requiring that roofs be constructed with fire-retardant materials. The club's favorite architect, though, was profoundly affected by the fire. Bernard Maybeck declared he would never again use wood as an exterior covering, one of his trademarks, and began experimenting with safer materials. Other improvements were made, as well, such as laying larger water mains and pipes, and Berkeley has never had a fire of that magnitude again.

There was, however, one final tragic consequence of the 1923 fire. In 1931, two teenagers found a gas pipe, which had been capped during the fire, in the basement of their home on Cedar Street. When the boys tried to tighten the cap, it burst and gas began filling the enclosed space. A small fire flared at the scene and firemen arrived quickly. But suddenly, a huge explosion shook the neighborhood, killing three people and injuring 70. Like a dying, angry dragon, the devastating fire of 1923 had reared its head and roared one last time.

North Berkeley after the fire of 1923. (PHOTO COURTESY OF BERKELEY HISTORICAL SOCIETY)

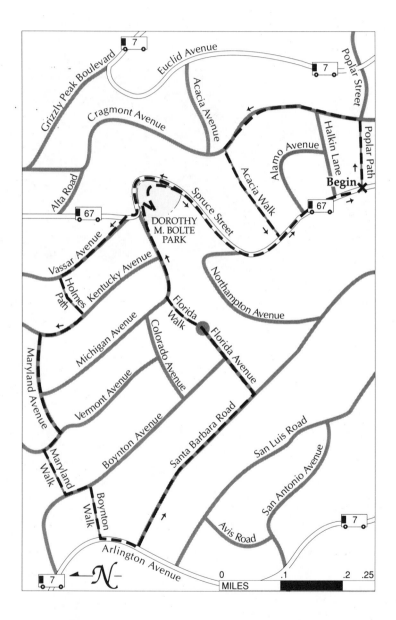

4
Walk of the States

Terrain: *easy to moderate; improved lanes and steps; unimproved paths*
Bus Line: *67*
Parks: *Dorothy M. Bolte, Tilden Regional*
Shops: *Walnut Square, Solano Avenue*
Distance: *2.5 miles*
Directions: *From University Avenue go north on Shattuck to Rose. Turn right to Spruce, then left past Marin Avenue, and just beyond Regal Road.*

In the far northern part of Berkeley, near its border with Kensington, is a newer neighborhood that names a number of its streets after states of the Union. You'll find a great park, views, and some surprisingly hidden paths and steps.

Start the walk on Spruce Street at the Poplar Path, which is just past Regal Road and signed on the eastern side of the street to the left of #747. Climb the concrete steps with white wooden rail to Cragmont Avenue, where you turn left on this quiet street past old Tudor Revivals and klinker brick, shingled cottages, like #752, continuing across Halkin Lane with more impressive Tudors on the right, noticing particularly the whimsical trim of #679 with its little cat cutout on the eaves above the doorway, and the shingled, brick cottage at #620.

Just beyond this house, the sidewalk on the west side starts looking like a path, and the sign for the Acacia Walk appears. Take this dirt path to the left, though a wonderland of toyon, birch, redwood, cedar, pine, and bay views, until it becomes all concrete and steps with a black wrought iron railing leading down to Spruce.

Go right on Spruce, trying to imagine this early street as it used to be in the late nineteenth century — as rolling hills and farm land. Cross where it's safest and after the street takes a horseshoe bend to the left, passing Bolte Park (we'll come back to this park later), look for Vassar Avenue on the left. Walk down Vassar just past the landscaped median strip to the Holmes Path, with a sign, to your left. This leads down to Kentucky, where a right takes you to Maryland which merges with Vermont.

Where Maryland Avenue meets Vermont Avenue, at the Vermont signpost, there are steep stairs heading down. This is the Maryland Walk, without its own sign. It leads to Boynton, where you jag left a short way to steps in the median strip and the continuation of the Maryland Walk (no sign but a white fire hydrant marks the spot).

This joins Arlington Avenue, where you turn left then in a short distance left again onto quieter Santa Barbara Road. Ascend Santa Barbara to the first street on your left, which is equally quiet Florida Avenue (although the sign is missing at this writing). A left on Florida takes you to the very hidden Florida Walk at the cul-de-sac at street's end (just past Boynton Avenue). There is a sign partially hidden by tree branches.

Mount the steep steps and lane of the Florida Walk to Michigan Avenue (it's name is etched in concrete at the top of the path), where you walk to the right to the Dorothy M. Bolte Park on your right. This used to be called Michigan Park, but was renamed in recognition of a long-time employee of the Berkeley Parks and Recreation Department.

To enter the park, and have a little fun in the process, find an asphalt path just past the last house on Michigan. Follow the path as it switches back and forth, finally reaching a bench and a giant concrete sliding board that funnels into an equally giant sand pit. The warning sign at the top of the slide is one of a kind, that, from personal observation, encourages that which it discourages: WARNING: DO NOT USE CARDBOARD OR OTHER MATERIALS TO INCREASE SPEED. I never would've thought of it.

There's also a craftsman jungle gym, complete with metal climbing pole, metal slide, and another large sand pit, enclosed with wood pilings and concrete blocks. And while any kids in tow play, you can bask in the sun (or fog) on a bench that overlooks the bay, the Berkeley Municipal Pier, and San Francisco's Sutro Tower.

From the park it's an easy jaunt down Spruce back to the Poplar Path beginnings of this North Berkeley walk.

Berkeley's Hillside Club

I n 1898, a group of women, who did not yet even have the right to vote, were outraged enough to storm Berkeley's elected trustees, the equivalent to the present city council. The town was growing and houses and roads began appearing in the quiet hills of Berkeley. In the words of one of the women, Mrs. Margaret Todd, the group "recognized the beauty of our hills and the awfulness of many of the houses. Its object was primarily to protect the hills of Berkeley from unsightly grading and the building of unsuitable and disfiguring houses; to do all in our power to beautify these hills and above all to create and encourage a decided opinion on these subjects."

They deemed Marin Avenue, one of the oldest streets in North Berkeley, unnecessarily steep, and when Cedar Street was laid out in the same fashion, "just like a city street, there was great consternation!" remembered Mrs. Todd. "Down to the Town Hall to protest to the Trustees."

The women felt strongly that the streets should follow the contours of the hills, winding gently and aesthetically, instead of skyrocketing like Marin. They even formalized their group into a club called the Hillside Club, dedicated to the protection and beautification of the hills. The town Trustees, however, were not impressed. "It seemed the Trustees were annoyed and said 'No,'" continued Mrs. Todd, quoted in the club's history. "They wouldn't plan the new streets as winding roads following the contours of the hills.

"The women were stopped for a short time. They decided to call on the men for help—invited them to a meeting at night. Women had no votes in those days—but their husbands had. That's the reason we have those lovely winding roads. They were winding all right and they can't be unwound."

Those husbands happened to include famed architect and urban planner Bernard Maybeck and John Galen Howard, the

architect who established the university's School of Architecture and who helped design the campus. Charles Keeler, a close confidant of Maybeck, author of *The Simple Home* and founder of the Berkeley Handicraft Guild, was active in the club, as well. They were advocates of simplicity in design, emphasizing "the need for beautiful and simple surroundings, the necessity of art in life," as Keeler wrote. They admired the romantic and picturesque street plans of noted California architect Frederick Law Olmstead, who designed New York's Central Park. And they rubbed elbows with naturalists John Muir and John Burroughs and landscape painter William Keith.

The club's yearbook of 1907–1908 was very specific as to what they wanted in the Berkeley Hills. "Roads should follow contour lines. . . . The steep parts can be handled in various ways, terraced in two levels as on Hearst Avenue, divided into narrow ways for driving with footpaths above and below and connecting steps for pedestrians." Much of North Berkeley today follows those guidelines thanks to this club, which is still intact as a social organization.

One early club pamphlet written in 1898 was entitled "What the Club Advocates" and stated its philosophy clearly: "The California hills are brown, therefore, the house should be brown. Redwood is the natural wood of the country, therefore, it is natural to use it. A house should not stand out in a landscape, but should fit in with it. This is the first principle that should govern the design of every house."

And the yearbook of 1906–1907 added, "Hillside Architecture is Landscape Gardening around a few rooms for use in case of rain."

That philosophy influenced the design of many of the pathways featured in this book. Mrs. Bertha Underhill, a longtime resident of Tamalpais Road and friend of the Maybeck family, remembers using the paths often when she was young, and meeting many neighbors along the way. But eventually as the century wore on, the automobile began to dominate, and use of the pathways dwindled. As a result, city maintenance funds began to dry up, and the condition of the paths suffered. Some are still landscaped by the city, but many signs have disappeared, concrete and asphalt are cracked, and a number are functionally unusable or undeveloped.

Yet most of the original pathways (and a number of Maybeck designed houses) still with us, offering models as to how construction can be in harmony with nature. Remember, and thank, the founding women of the Hillside Club when you walk these paths.

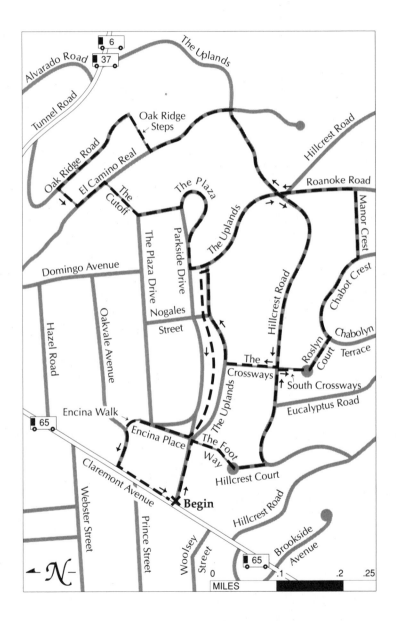

5

Claremont Crossways & Cul-de-Sacs

Terrain: *easy to steep; improved lanes and steps, unimproved trails*
Bus Lines: *65, 6, or 37*
Parks: *John Muir School playground at Claremont near Ashby*
Shops: *Claremont Avenue at The Uplands, College Avenue, Domingo Street*
Distance: *3 miles*
Directions: *Take Claremont Avenue exit off Route 24 and go left off exit; or Ashby Avenue exit off I-80 to College Avenue. Turn right to Claremont then left to The Uplands.*

After the San Francisco earthquake and fire in 1906, San Franciscans began looking for safer places to live. With the building of the majestic Claremont Hotel a few years later, along with the Key Route electric train extension up Claremont Avenue, the Elmwood-Claremont section of town began to draw the attention of land developers. Nestled in the foothills, it presented good views, gentle elevation, convenience to the ferry in West Berkeley, and proximity to the university.

From a few huge estates, Mason-McDuffie Realtors creatively subdivided the area, and their top landscape architect, Frederick Law Olmstead, famous for his designs in New York and Yosemite, designed the street plan. They called it Claremont Park and built homes suitable to the conservative tastes of their businessmen clients from the city. Unlike the shingled, rustic look in North Berkeley, architects like John Hudson Thomas used stucco, which conveyed a more stately appearance, although there were experiments with progressive forms. Today, in this highly desirable neighborhood, the trees are mature, the houses weathered, Harwood Creek is visible in places, and the entire area has a settled feeling, ripened by age and care.

Start this walk at Claremont Avenue and The Uplands. Great stone pillars, with large lamps on top, mark the entrance to this section — pillars meant to decorate and give a sense of identity to Claremont Park. Large spruce, maple, and oak line the street as well.

Follow The Uplands and climb the steep steps, known as the Foot Way, appearing shortly on the right (they are unmarked but its iron railing makes them easy to spot). The steps become a path, complete with Victorian lamppost and an assortment of interesting fences, and exits onto Hillcrest Court, a cul-de-sac with three representative examples of Claremont's first houses. John Hudson Thomas, a popular architect of the day, designed the Tudor Revival at #2, the stylish stucco at #10, and the avant-garde design at #12. That wonderful Bay Area mix of maples and palms complete the design of the street.

Go left on Hillcrest Road, viewing the impressive red brick mansion straight ahead at #120 with its lone palm landscaping the front lawn. Brick is humankind's oldest building material, but as we saw from the destructive earthquake in 1989, old brick structures are vulnerable to strong tremors.

Pass Eucalyptus Road and cross the street and find The South Crossways, a path, with a sign, just past #142, that gently descends past a jungle of gardens and mini-forests, joining another cul-de-sac, Rosyln Court. Within a total of a few hundred feet, zigzag left onto Chablyn Court, then right on Chabot Crest, then left on Manor Crest.

Climb Roanoke Road to the left to the five corners where Roanoke, Hillcrest, and The Uplands meet. Continue right on The Uplands, past canopies of laurel and ginkgo trees to El Camino Real, where you walk left past a small grove of graceful birches. As the street bends to the right, look for steps to your right, marked by an iron railing and post (where a sign used to be), just beyond #99.

These are the steep Oak Ridge Steps, lined with oak and cedar, transporting you up to Oak Ridge Road. You can only go left on Oak Ridge, where a short walk will lead you to a set of un-named steps on the left, just after #50 and next to a concrete lamppost and white fire hydrant. It's across from a Beaux–Arts inspired mansion on the right.

Drop back to El Camino Real, where you turn left, walking a short way to steps called The Cutoff, on your right. There is a sign here, but just in case it's taken down in the future, as so many others have been, The Cutoff starts just after #62.

Two classic houses flank The Cutoff at the bottom where it meets The Plaza Drive. John Hudson Thomas designed a very vertical house at #95 to the right, with Italian cypress, added later, accentuating its height. On the left are the natural tones of the Gertrude White House designed by Harris Allen in 1913.

Turn left onto The Plaza Drive. This leads to Parkside Drive and a small, yet elegant park/cul-de-sac called The Plaza (locals call it Round Park), with luxurious palms and pines, a magnificent birch, and more finely crafted homes built in the early twentieth century. Circle the park, then go up a few steps on your left and turn left onto The Uplands.

At the top, continue right onto Hillcrest, past ivy-covered homes with intricate windy steps, to an antique lamppost on your right and six metal poles to block vehicles from entering the path. It's just past #151 with its unique brick column and wood slat fence. This is The Crossways (a paved ramp suitable for wheelchairs) where you turn right and descend the privet-

and redwood-lined path to The Uplands. From here, there are fine views of the hills and the Claremont Hotel.

Go right to a crosswalk where the street bends to the right, cross carefully as cars usually travel quite fast here, take a few steps down, and turn left on a dirt path. This unnamed path, though right in between Parkside Drive and The Uplands, has the feel of a woodland trail, with acacias, mixed conifers, redwoods, toyons, bay laurels, and live oaks. It becomes all pine at one point—a beautiful grove of Ponderosa pine—then a small stand of second-generation redwoods, until you exit this unlikely forest at the junction of Parkside, The Uplands, and Encina Place.

Cross and bear right on Encina Place, past houses with expansive gardens, ponds, streams, buckeye trees, and redwoods (the beauties at #6 and #10 were built in 1906, designed by the well-known and influential First Bay Tradition architect, Ernest Coxhead), to the Encina Walk on your left, just past the old Tudor cottage at #2.

A stop on the bridge allows a look at the rustic 1912 log house, the waters of Harwood Creek flowing below, and the deep green leaf, red-berry holly tree on the bank. There's a huge redwood at the exit, where you go left onto Oak Vale Avenue, then to busy Claremont, and left, back to the entry pavilions of Claremont Park at The Uplands. It's a neighborhood that is as elegant today as when it was developed.

Berkeley Cats

*T*o know Berkeley is to know its cats. In fact, to know Berkeley people just observe their cats, or that they have no cats, or that they take their cats for Sunday drives in the family Volvo station wagon. There *are* Berkeley people who have dogs instead of cats, but with dogs you can tell the physiognomy of their owners rather than their psychology. I know an elderly man who yaps and waddles right along with his little mutzies, but I couldn't say I really know him.

Cats reveal the tucked-away threads of people's lives, and, so, the true fabric of a community. Some move in cautious ways. Others are bold, brassy types who prance up as you walk by, rub up against your leg, and practically invite you in for tea. Then there are those who hide out behind the house, even behind the garage, peeking out, dreading the possibility of approaching footsteps. Their owners, too, are behind the living room curtains peering out through the slit, hardly breathing, waiting, worrying, wishing the interlopers away. Or how about those slinky longhairs who sidle up and turn so easily, so willingly, on their backs, seducing each passerby who takes the time to stop, reach down, and give a kitzle behind the ears. Their owners can often be found puttering around the front yard, greeting everyone in sight.

Then, of course, there are the daredevils—those stunt cats who dart across the street, attack a tree, leaping ten feet in one lunge, then fall and follow a passerby for a block or so, creating the inherited-stray illusion, one of the oldest cat-versus-person tricks in the book. Look for the red Mustang convertible outside these houses with a Grateful Dead sticker on the rear window. The owners of these cats can often be found at Chinese restaurants ordering dishes marked "hot and spicy," or can be seen at sidewalk cafes with large tropical birds on their shoulders.

Finally, there's that cat—usually a domestic shorthair—who

sits most of the day on an elevated spot near the sidewalk in warm weather and inside the front window in cold, watching the passing scene, alert, aware, sensitive, a correct cat in every way, not too timid, not too forward, not too needy, not too aloof—a cat who would rather be alone or with its own kind than ingratiate itself at the foot of some human. A savvy cat who knows something of life, who's been around, as they say, who's tasted the milk and the meat, the boudoir and the street, who doesn't respond right away when called, lifting an eyelid to see if the call is worth heeding—a cat who sees the mouse but merely records a memo in her mental notebook for future reference, who doesn't take anything at face value but who considers and weighs the implications—a cat who mulls it over before acting. A cat's cat.

You may have to search for these cats on your walks. Their spots are usually private ones where they groom themselves often but don't make a show of it. They seem to love routine, sitting day in and day out in the same place. But this is all part of the no-change game that makes people think of them as boring and just not worth the time to seek out. The owners of these cats rarely have their houses robbed, seem chronically unemployed, but always have enough money. They are often divorced and happy. They order out for pizza a lot, have their morning coffee on popular Berkeley street corners, and write off every waking minute on their tax returns, never seeming to get audited.

So, you see, to know a town you must observe its cats very closely. Unlike dogs who come slobbering up to you totally open and direct, cats have their enigmatic ways. You can't pin them down from day to day. You can't predict the direction a cat will go, or when it will go, or who it will go with. But cats, themselves, know exactly what's happening and, as a result, have Berkeley sewed up. They even have their own master plan and everything's right on schedule. In fact, I would say that Berkeley is what it is today because of its cats. That's a bold statement, I know. But facts are facts. And cats are cats.

Oh, there is one other kind of cat. It is that rare breed that has never lost its kittenish ways—the eternal player, that over-40-month-old whom the cat food manufacturers officially refer to as "a mature adult" but who still chases its tail, gets excited by water flushing down the toilet, and licks necks as if still nursing. This cat, despite advancing years, will jump six feet straight up to swat a dangling wire, goes ga-ga over birds and butterflies and loves to "help" make the bed by diving under the sheets as they waft down. She cares little for the nuts and bolts of being a cat—the workaday cat world of taking little bites at a time, short naps, and periodic grooming. This cat plays like hell then poops out for a few hours. The owners of such cats generally enjoy life. They play a lot, of course. They smile and laugh a lot, and they rest often. They can be seen, at times, picking plums from neighborhood trees, almost never washing their cars, and grabbing a few hours, here and there, to write books like this one.

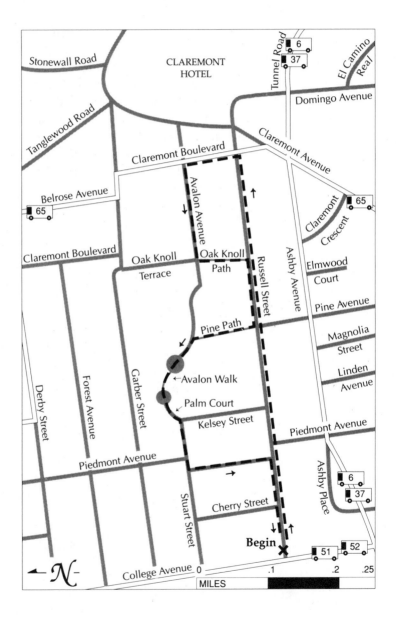

6
Of Pine & Oak & Elmwood

Terrain: *easy; improved paths and steps*
Bus Lines: *51, 52, 6, 17, or 37*
Parks: *Willard Park at Hillegass and Derby; Alta Bates Hospital Park, off Regent near Prince*
Shops: *College Avenue between Russell and Webster*
Distance: *1.5 miles*
Directions: *From I-80, take Ashby Avenue exit and continue to College Avenue. Turn left to Russell Street.*

The Elmwood section is one of Berkeley's safest, most easily walked, and most elegantly landscaped neighborhoods. It was first laid out in 1905 and has matured well. Here the terrain is gentle, the houses distinctive, and the paths and lanes perfect for a pleasant weekend stroll or a fast, before dinner hike. It's an area that reminds me of tidy, picturesque towns in the heartland of Holland.

This is a relatively short walk that begins on Russell Street just east of College Avenue. Walk up Russell's mild grade, admiring homes, gardens, views of the Claremont Hotel, and many tree species such as redwood, pine, palm, plum, poplar, cypress, birch, maple, and the tree that gave the neighborhood its name, the elm. These trees are about 100 years old and currently do not have Dutch elm disease, which has virtually wiped out the elm on the East Coast. But, according to the department in charge of maintaining Berkeley's trees, eventually all the elms in the Bay Area will die since there is no known way to stop the beetle that spreads the disease from tree to tree. When a tree needs to be removed, the city consults with local residents before deciding on an appropriate replacement species.

Continuing up Russell, notice, too, the stylish, flowing Mediterranean design of #2827, and the Greek Revival mansion at #2959, with its Corinthian columns and ivy-covered wall. At the top, go left onto Claremont Boulevard, through the brick and iron gateway that was designed by John Galen Howard in 1907 as the entrance to the Claremont Court subdivision at that time. The mansion on the immediate left was built in 1912. Go left on Avalon Avenue, first looking across Claremont Boulevard at the classy Julia Morgan original at #2821 on the corner, combining Beaux Arts and Georgian styles with a Mission red-tile roof.

In a short while, on this street lined with liquidambar and maple trees, go left again on the Oak Knoll Path. It starts at a lamppost, opposite the street, Oak Knoll Terrace, and just before the inviting house at #2934 with its First Bay Tradition features. Follow the path, flanked by cypress, magnolia, and ivy fences, back to Russell where you turn right.

Soon, on your right, will appear the brick border of the Magnes Museum, a fascinating collection of Jewish history and culture, that offers a good side trip if you have the time. Its grounds alone make for a pleasant walk through well-maintained gardens, redwoods, palms, picnic tables, stone sculptures, monuments, and memorials.

Continuing down Russell, go right on the Pine Path, which is opposite Pine Street, past #2901, and marked by a sign. Saunter along its pink concrete path and steps, under oak, pine, and toyon, onto Avalon and go left to a cul-de-sac. Look for the sign at the end pointing to the Avalon Walk and savor brown-shingled and brick houses and views of Mt. Tamalpais in Marin along the pink concrete way.

These steps lead to Palm Court, which quickly becomes Stuart Street. Follow Stuart to Piedmont Avenue, where you turn left, past sycamores and California bungalows and brown-shingled houses with broad gardens and grounds that would have pleased Charles Keeler. Go right on Russell and back to College.

If you still have time and the interest, head a few blocks north on College between Derby Street and Dwight Way, where you can see several more houses and a church designed by Julia Morgan, who was a student of Maybeck's and the first woman to be accepted into the famous, though, at that time, male chauvinistic, Ecole des Beaux Arts in Paris. She did this by disguising herself as a man and passing all the entrance tests, thus making it impossible for the intimidated architectural school to turn her away. Her most famous project was the fabulous Hearst Castle in San Simeon on the central coast of California. Locally, in a section the Berkeley Architectural Heritage Association calls Julia Morgan Park, this highly sought after architect designed the St. John's Presbyterian Church in 1908 at #2640 College (now the Julia Morgan Theater), #2740, #2742, #2814, #2816 Derby in 1907, #2608 Warring Street in 1914, as well as #2629, #2616, #2618, #2531, #2535, #2539, #2514, and #2525 Etna Street in 1905. Maybeck designed #2515 Etna Street for early Sierra Club naturalist and photographer Cedric Wright (see page 144) in 1921.

The commercial buildings on College between Russell and Ashby Avenue are historically significant as well. Most were built in the early twentieth century.

Berkeley's First Environmental Activist

*B*erkeley's Bernard Maybeck was known for his environmentally sensitive architecture and pathway designs, but his wife may well be remembered as the town's first environmental activist. One day, just after the turn of the century, when Berkeley was hopping with residential developers and street planners, Mrs. Maybeck happened upon a gang of city workmen ready to fell a native live oak tree in the middle of Le Roy Avenue. She and her husband were founding members of the town's Hillside Club, whose stated creed was to "encourage the making of parks and playgrounds and the planting of trees within the city limits, to beautify the streets, gardens, and homes within said city . . ." And from another of its members, Mrs. Frank Morton Todd, "The few native trees that have survived centuries of fire and flood lived because they had chosen the best places. They should be jealously preserved. Bend the road, divide the lots, place the houses to accommodate them!"

Although not exactly an Earth First! monkeywrencher, Annie White Maybeck, with Hillside Club battle cries in mind, advanced on the crew, talked the men into waiting a bit before they chopped the tree, commandeered a buckboard wagon, raced to city hall, and convinced the trustees to spare the tree. The original tree has died, but today, on Le Roy, between Ridge and Le Conte, a young live oak still grows, thanks to Annie Maybeck, in the middle of the street!

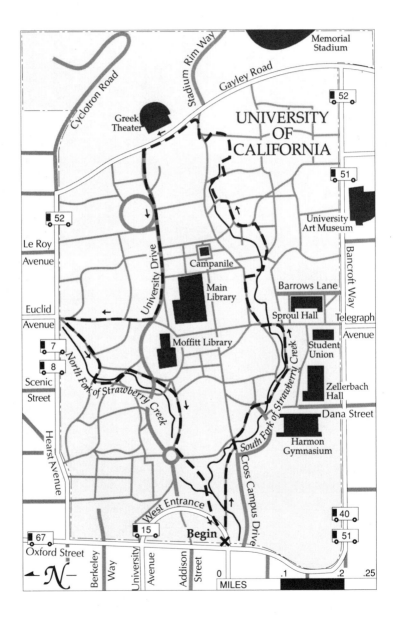

7

The Campus Creek Walk

Terrain: *easy; improved paths and bridges*
Bus Lines: *52 or 67*
Parks: *UC Botanical Gardens (in Strawberry Canyon, above the stadium, near the Lawrence Hall of Science)*
Shops: *Downtown Berkeley, ASUC store in student union building, Bancroft and Telegraph Avenues*
Distance: *2.5 miles*
Directions: *At top of University Avenue, turn right on Oxford Street.*

The University of California was the hub, wheel and spokes of early Berkeley. Its buildings and landscape reflect a tranquil time when people got to places a bit slower, allowing enjoyment of the idyllic environment of the campus. The pace may be quicker now, but you can still see students sauntering under Sather Gate, sitting by the cool waters of Strawberry Creek, or studying on the grass at Faculty Glade.

Since the college's founding in the mid-nineteenth century, there's been Free Speech and tear gas and animal rights and South African protests, but the creek and the pines and the redwoods haven't changed much. Most of the buildings and landscape design came after 1902 when a Parisian architect, Emile Benard, won a $10,000 prize for his design. American architect John Galen Howard supervised the development of the grounds, keeping the essential French academic influence, but adding his own touches, like retaining the free and wild feeling of the north and south forks of Strawberry Creek and adding the rustic, and emphatically American, Senior Men's Hall to the European flavor.

This walk begins near the campus's west entrance on Oxford Street just across from Center Street. The itinerary of this loop is to follow the course of both forks of Strawberry Creek throughout the campus. On a sidewalk just south of the entrance, cross a bridge and follow the path which bears right along the south fork of the creek. Pass the Alumni House on the right, with the creek and its orderly stone embankment on the left. An arched stone bridge allows a good view of small waterfalls up stream before the path exits at Sather Gate just north of Sproul Plaza and the Student Union.

Proceed under the Gate and over the bridge, bearing right to pick up the path again. Opposite red-bricked South Hall to the left, take the red brick steps to the right, and down to the wooden bridge. Instead of using this handsome bridge, though, turn left, and cross the next wooden bridge. Pass the Japanese-influenced columns of Anthony Hall and go left toward Stephens Hall, soon coming to Hamilton Grove, a tasteful mingling of redwoods and benches, heralding the entrance to Faculty Glade, a hilly expanse of lawn and live oaks, adjacent to the Faculty Club. This building was designed by Bernard Maybeck in the style of the California missions, with tiled roof, arched openings, a campanile tower, and, in true Maybeck fashion, a brown-shingled second story. The Glade is a good place for lunch in the sun or, on a hot day, in the shade of one of its welcoming trees.

Continue on the path, traversing a bridge, keeping the Faculty Club to your right and soon passing one of the most interesting buildings in Berkeley if not the entire state. It is a magnificent redwood log structure, surrounded by large redwoods. It is the Senior Men's Hall, completed in 1906 and

designed by John Galen Howard. It was commissioned by the prestigious Secret Order of the Golden Bear for their headquarters. (See page 62 for more on this building.)

Bear right, past the log hall, then past the Women's Faculty Club on the left, up a few stone steps to a parking lot. Walk left through the lot, then right toward a redwood grove.

Gayley Road is up ahead, but before reaching it, veer around the faculty children's playground and walk toward the Campanile, noticing the creek on the left. For a side diversion, you can ride the elevator to the Campanile's observation tower to hear its 12 bells more clearly and see the great view. The tower was financed by Jane Krom Sather (and is officially called Sather Tower) with John Galen Howard designing it in 1914. Its bells came from England in 1917 on a ship that ran a German submarine blockade. The sturdy tower was constructed with earthquakes in mind.

This is the eastern end of University Drive, which transects the entire campus. Follow this street past Evans and Campbell Halls, then past the barracks-like buildings of the counseling and placement centers, obviously not designed by Mr. Howard or, I hope, any of his students.

Just beyond these buildings, opposite the Main Library, take the path to the right, leading up and past the Earth Sciences building, to North Gate. It's here, to the left, down a street marked "Not a Through Way," that you'll pick up the north fork of Strawberry Creek on the right.

Cross the first wooden bridge you come to, then go up the stone steps, and turn left to walk along the creek. In a short way, go left across the next wooden bridge, then turn right along the creek, past virgin coast redwoods the size of some of those in Muir Woods in Marin County. Some of these trees live more than 2,000 years and exceed 360 feet. At one time, before extensive logging, they occupied 1,250,000 acres within 30 miles of the coast.

Cross University Drive, near Moffit Library, and stay left. Follow the stone-embanked creek, which snakes through the lawn area in front of the Biochemistry/Psychology building.

Just past a small waterfall, the creek then goes underground until it surfaces in the Eucalyptus Grove on the left. Eucalyptus seed was sent here from Australia as early as 1856, mainly to be used as a fast-growing source of hardwood for wood trim, fine furniture, and cabinet making. The whole enterprise collapsed when it was found it grew much slower here than Down Under. The tree was abandoned commercially, but by 1871, the price of eucalyptus trees had dropped to between 10 and 25 cents each, which is why so many were planted. Early community groups, like the Berkeley Floral Society, also encouraged the planting of the many deciduous and evergreen trees, like silver-leaf maple and acacia, we see on streets today.

You're now at the point where you started this walk, which

is also the junction of the north and south forks of Strawberry Creek. A plaque near the creek commemorates the arrival at that spot, on March 27, 1772, of a scientific team, the Don Pedro Fages Expedition, sent by the emperor of Spain to find a land route to northern California. They were the first white men to explore what was to become Berkeley. Four years later, Juan Bautista de Anza founded the settlement of San Francisco, still looking for the elusive land route north.

At that time, salmon were spawning in Strawberry Creek, but now it surfaces in only one other spot, Strawberry Creek Park in West Berkeley, before draining into the bay near the marina. Groups like the Urban Creeks Council and Berkeley Citizens for Creek Restoration, however, are lobbying to resurrect parts of the creek in the downtown district. The latter group has stenciled the names of all of the town's 14 creeks, with city council's approval, on sidewalks and curbs above their underground locations — an environmental map showing walkers 860 places where creeks flow beneath and once coursed freely above.

UC Berkeley's Senior Men's Hall

Near the Maybeck-designed Men's Faculty Club is a log building that may be the most unusual on campus, and one of the rarest of its kind in the state. The Senior Men's Hall was commissioned in 1906 by the Order of the Golden Bear (OGB), which was, at that time, an all-senior, male secret society. Membership was based on student service and social status, and their rustic headquarters building was a symbol of senior control on campus.

The building was designed by the university's supervising architect and head of the department, John Galen Howard, who completely departed from the French academic architectural influence evident on the rest of the campus he helped conceive. As the campus grew, all student organizations eventually used the hall until the Student Union was built.

One part of the building that was off-limits to everyone but members of the OGB was its second, concealed room, connected to the main, public room by a low, secret passage and divided by a huge stone fireplace with two hearths, one in each room. This smaller, east room was where the Secret Order met, and one can only imagine the pomp and circumstance surrounding its leaders as they sat on the raised podium with three regal chairs in front of its frosted glass window.

This went on until 1973 when the cabin was closed for safety reasons. The year before, university officials planned to raze the building to make space for a dining annex to be used jointly by the Men's and Women's Faculty Clubs. But sentiment to preserve the building was high, and two women, Sylvia McLaughlin and Lesley Emmington (again, it was women who acted first to save a part of Berkeley's heritage), started a Save Senior Men's Hall campaign. Students, faculty, administrators, and alumni joined in and succeeded in not only stopping the demolition but getting the building listed with the National Register of

Historic Places in 1974. The campaign to save it also led to the founding of the Berkeley Architectural Heritage Association (BAHA), which has been actively cataloging and protecting historically significant structures in Berkeley ever since.

Though preserved, the log Men's Hall sat unused for a number of years until the OGB, now open to women and no longer secret, raised $50,000 in 1985 for cosmetic improvements to the "secret" meeting room and the addition of a wheelchair access ramp. The club uses the building occasionally for its monthly meetings and receptions after football games and hopes to eventually complete structural renovations on this rare example of state exposition and park structures. It's one of the few that hasn't been demolished.

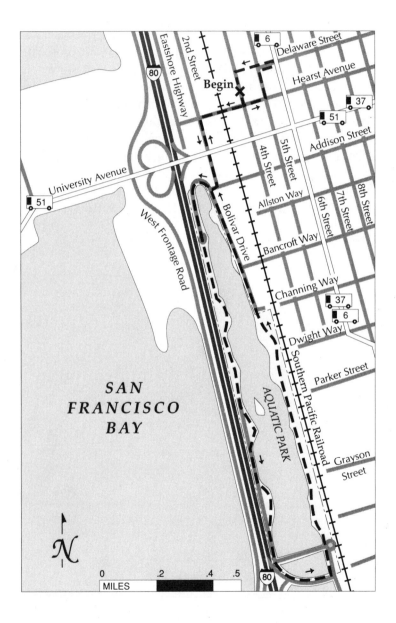

8

Oceanview & a Hundred-Acre Park

Terrain: *easy; improved and unimproved paths*
Bus Lines: *51M*
Parks: *Aquatic, Berkeley Marina, Adventure Playground (on University Avenue just before the Recreation Pier)*
Shops: *Fourth and Hearst Streets*
Distance: *4.7 miles*
Directions: *From I-80, take University Avenue exit. Then a left on Sixth Street and another left on Hearst to Fourth Street.*

The Oceanview area in West Berkeley was the site of the first settlement in town, along with the first business. It's still a major commercial area, but over the past few years there's been a residential revival, featuring creative, fairly affordable housing. There are interesting shops, great restaurants, building supply companies, outlet stores, light industrial factories, and an attractive senior center. In the daytime it's a relatively safe area to walk, and with a side street connector, links up with Aquatic Park, a little-used lake and loop walk, that is part bird sanctuary, part water sports wonderland, part picnicking grounds, all sandwiched between Interstate 80 on the west and the Southern Pacific tracks and trains on the east.

Start on Fourth Street and go right on Hearst Street toward

the railroad tracks. Continue across the tracks, being cautious to heed any red flashing signal at this active track, turning left on Second Street. It was at this corner, where a building supply firm now operates, that John Everding opened the first industrial enterprise in Berkeley in 1855: the Pioneer Starch and Grist Mill. But Ohlone Indians had been living there for centuries before Everding arrived, for one of the largest Indian mounds in the area was discovered on this site as well.

Walking under University Avenue, go right at Addison Street and enter Aquatic Park, a 99.36-acre park that was developed by the Works Projects Administration (WPA) during the Depression. The road that circles most of the park is Bolivar Drive.

Bear right at Bolivar, keeping the lake on your left. You'll see coots, mallards, goldeneyes, gulls, egrets, herons, and geese. You'll also hear the constant roar of traffic on the freeway, but in my experience, the noise is so consistent and the action on the lake so engrossing that the traffic noise is not a major distraction.

Soon Bolivar bars cars for a stretch and a dirt path hugs the shoreline in spots. The waterfowl seem less skittish even as kayakers and canoeists glide by. A little farther, cars can rejoin Bolivar, but the path along the shore becomes more continuous so you can avoid the vehicles (although there really aren't many of them on this road, nor do they travel fast). The lagoon at the southern end of the lake was originally intended for sailing model sailboats but has, instead, become a quiet sanctuary for birds wanting to escape the wake of weekend waterskiers.

Continue around the lagoon on a path which circumscribes most of it. The lagoon and lake are fed by creeks as well as a breakwater system, now under I-80, that allows bay water to enter. This area was basically wetlands and marsh before the WPA project began.

At the eastern end of the lagoon, pass the headquarters for the International Bird Rescue Center, a group that tries to save injured waterfowl and seabirds — most often birds soaked in oil after tanker spills at sea. They wash each bird in a grease-cutting detergent, releasing back into the wild those they can save. This dedicated center has been able to rescue many birds this way.

The eastern shore of Aquatic Park is just for hikers, bikers, and Frisbee throwers. An asphalt path winds through willow, cedar, acacia, and eucalyptus, crosses a few small streams, passes a number of picnic tables and barbecues, and is farther from the freeway, making it quieter than the west side. The path eventually leads you right along the water, until returning to Addison.

Before reaching Addison, though, check out the mini-farm at Bancroft Way, the only other street providing direct access to the park. Here you'll find caged chickens, pheasants, peacocks, guinea hens, turkeys, pigeons, ducks, geese, and lots of babies of various species. If you have kids, this will be a high point.

At Addison go right then left on Second, the same way you came (there's an excellent winery at this corner, Audubon Cellars, which, as of this writing, has a tasting bar and donates a portion of each sale to the Audubon Society).

Turn right on Hearst, continuing past Fourth to Fifth Street, where you turn left. A half-block on your right perambulate around the wooden walkway of the unique Delaware Historical Development with its nineteenth-century feel. You can also see some of the innovative low- to moderate-income homes on Fifth Street, a model development getting national attention for its creative design and affordability.

Return to Fourth Street via a path directly opposite the Historical Development. When the village of Ocean View started, you would have been covered in dust and caked in mud after such a walk, so give a point to modern improvements.

Ocean View:
Berkeley's First Settlement

B erkeley's origins can be found at the mouth of Strawberry Creek, where a Dutch emigre, James Jacobs, began anchoring his sloop in 1853 to facilitate his freighter business. The fresh water was good for the boat's hull, the rent was free, and the location ideal for doing business around the bay. He liked it so much, the next year he built a wharf and began constructing a house. For many years, this area, at the foot of Delaware Street, was known as Jacob's Landing [sic].

Not long after Jacobs, Massachusetts native Captain William Bowen returned from the gold fields and established an inn in the same area on Contra Costa Road (now San Pablo Avenue), running it for 23 years as it became a regular stop on the stagecoach line.

Others followed, particularly entrepreneurs discouraged by the lack of good water and the high costs in San Francisco. A starch and grist mill set up shop as the first manufacturing business. A soap company started, complete with paddle-wheel ferry. And a lumberyard followed, started by Zimri Heywood, a Mainer who survived three wives, brought his 13 children with him to California, found a fourth wife to help care for them, and raised a family of which two sons and a grandson went on to become the equivalent of mayors of Berkeley .

A few small farms sprung up around Ocean View, as the area was now called, and the community took root. The Ocean View School was founded. A planing mill began cranking out decorative and functional building essentials demanded by a growing late-nineteenth-century American community. There was even a brewery that serviced a beer garden called Willow Grove Park near the present Spenger's Restaurant.

With the growth of the university and Berkeley proper, Ocean

View started to be known as West Berkeley but maintained its separate identity from the "college crowd" to the east. A state law, in 1873, banned the consumption of alcohol within a mile of the university, which led to the growth of taverns in Ocean View to service the dry Berkeley two miles away. At one point there were 28 bars in the area, and the crime rate, including public drunkenness, soared. West Berkeley residents felt animosity toward their "holier than thou" neighbors to the east, who pointed a finger of blame for a problem that started with the demand they created.

But despite the hard feelings, the two towns, through the help of nondenominational Christian societies and fraternal organizations, finally acknowledged their interdependence and successfully petitioned the legislature to incorporate in 1878. They acted just in time, for the city of Oakland was breathing down their necks wanting to annex the area and its $10 million in taxable property.

Political and social divisions persisted though, and today, West Berkeley flatlanders, predominantly working class, sometimes deride the gentry up in "the hills." There are good, relatively affordable houses and fewer rowdy bars, making the Oceanview/West Berkeley section one of those up-and-coming neighborhoods, as it was in 1853 after Jim Jacobs arrived.

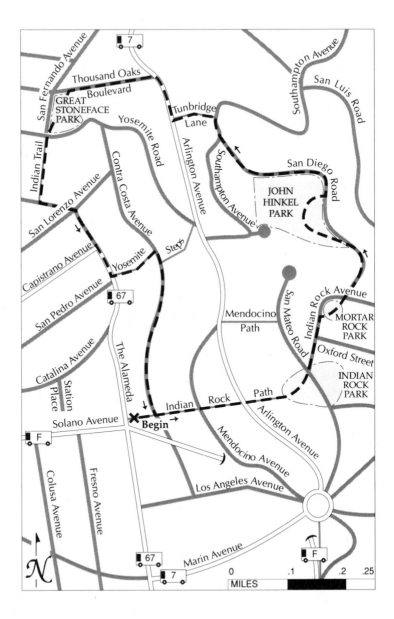

9

Indian Rocks & Four Parks

Terrain: *easy to moderate; improved lanes and steps, unimproved paths*

Bus Lines: *67 or 7*

Parks: *Indian Rock, Mortar Rock, John Hinkel, Old Stoneface, Thousand Oaks School*

Shops: *Solano Avenue*

Distance: *2.5+ miles*

Directions: *From I-80, take University Avenue exit to Martin Luther King Way. Turn left and continue to The Alameda and Solano Avenue.*

The Ohlone Indians, Berkeley's first inhabitants, would not at first recognize the town's Thousand Oaks section, but after following this walk they might remember some of the rocks and streams, the oaks and redwoods, the vistas and topography.

Solano Avenue and its commercial development was the harbinger of this section of North Berkeley, and old photographs show the street with the open hills and scattered oak trees above. Landscape architect Mark Daniels was responsible for the design of the area's parks and paths, and Maybeck, Morgan, Henry Gutterson, and other top architects of the day crafted many of the houses, contributing to the area's popularity then and now. Mason-McDuffie Realtors developed the first subdivision in the area and called it Northbrae. This is one of the longest walks in this book, offering much diversity in natural and cultural history. With its ancient boulders, varied parks, and hidden pathways, it's also a lot of fun.

Start at the Indian Rock Path at the northeast corner of The Alameda and Solano Avenue. Walk up this long, straight gentle path past bright gardens set off by white stucco entrance ways draped with morning-glories and even graffiti on a bare wall. Leave the busy intersection, crossing sleepy Contra Costa and Mendocino Avenues, past busy Arlington Avenue, finally reaching the mammoth boulder, Indian Rock and its surrounding park. This rock, between 9 and 12 million years old, is part of the ash deposits from volcanic activity farther north that also formed Grizzly Peak higher in the hills.

It's fairly soft as rocks go, so I wouldn't advise ropes and pitons, but if you go to the right, you'll find spiraling stone steps that have been etched into the rock face, allowing an easy walk up. The rock is used by free-climbing rock climbers, training their muscles for steeper Sierra adventures.

When you're finished absorbing the expansive bay view, find another set of inlaid steps behind you on the eastern side of the rock and descend this precipitous route carefully. A water fountain greets you at the base, and across the street is the rest of Indian Rock Park, with huge eucalyptus trees, stone seats, picnic tables, coast live oak trees, and a stately redwood set among flowers blooming nearly year-round.

Before you get too comfortable though, keep in mind there are three more superb parks ahead. From here bear left onto Indian Rock Avenue and continue to the smaller Mortar Rock Park. This is Indian Rock's baby sibling, deposited by the same ancient volcanic activity. Enter and bear right to stone steps leading to the top. You still get a bay view here but the surrounding laurels and live oaks keep it fairly focused.

Mortar Rock derives its name from the small craters in the

lower stones. Early Ohlone women laboriously pounded acorns, gathered from the oak trees, with stone pestles, creating mortars in the rocks. It was part of a daily process which produced a fine meal that eventually became breakfast. These tribes supposedly ate 1,000 to 2,000 pounds of acorns a year, so Mortar Rock must have been as popular as Peet's Coffee.

Descend on the north side and continue along adjacent San Diego Road where the sidewalk quickly turns to a dirt path and more coast live oaks. Shortly on your left, after a sprawling estate, are trails leading into one of Berkeley's treasures, John Hinkel Park. There's a majestic stone and wood bench on one trail near the top, with a telescopic bay view — a good place to stop and have lunch or write a dissertation. Continue, noticing the amphitheater below, where an annual Shakespeare series has been held. Then suddenly, enter a thick forest of native plants and trees.

This park is worth exploring, which is easy to do since the city has improved the paths and added attractive redwood handrails throughout the four-plus acres of ground. A section of Blackberry Creek, one of the few places in town to see a creek in its natural setting, flows and falls through the heart of the park, with oak and bay laurel abounding.

Climbing the steps next to the creek, leave the park and follow San Diego as it bends left past a tamer entrance to the park and a meeting hall, built in 1911 and available to the public by reservation. The red-tile roof at #754 is one where each tile was shaped on the roofer's thigh. It's the way things were done in 1926. Continue to Southampton Avenue, looking for Tunbridge Lane, marked by a sign a short distance on the left. Head west to fine views, terraced gardens, flower-bordered lawns, and, finally, Arlington, where you can hear, and imagine, the north branch of Capistrano Creek flowing hidden under the concrete.

Cross Arlington and go right to Thousand Oaks Boulevard, turn left, noticing the Julia Morgan–designed house at #1937, and proceed to San Fernando Avenue, where The Great Stoneface Park greets you. Archaeologists have found evidence of Indian habitation at this site, and today there's a wide inviting lawn and a huge boulder with many faces but no steps up. To the right of the park, by the way, look for a white picket fence and house that look like they were shipped whole from a New England village.

When you're through trying out the lawn, traverse the park from east to west to the signpost San Fernando and Yosemite Road. Just across the street see another sign reading "Indian Trail." Put your moccasins on and descend — slowly.

The Indian Trail was probably just that at one time; now it's still as functional, and one of the most singular of Berkeley's paths. Old stone steps, moss-covered walls, gardens and gates, curves and bends almost usher you into reading rooms of elegant brick homes. It ends too soon as it meets The Alameda, an ancient stone urn gracing the junction.

Now go left and continue on The Alameda past Capistrano Avenue, where again you can hear the underground creek, to the Yosemite Steps, marked with a sign at this writing but, if the sign disappears, next to a telephone pole and a sprawling pine tree. Scale the steps, past low fences and varied backyard acreage, to Contra Costa, turn right and stop at the iron road guards. Below, through the brake, is a branch of Codornices Creek which you can see from the west side of the street. Even in midsummer, this creek, fed by underground springs, still runs.

Farther along this quiet street is Indian Rock Path once again, but before returning, take a moment to admire the Japanese garden next to the path on the other side of the street. It might help keep your mind tranquil as you reenter the busy world of upper Solano Avenue and The Alameda. Then maybe you can imagine peaceful Marin Creek as the Ohlone Indians knew it. Today, it flows almost the entire length of Solano Avenue underground.

"February in Berkeley"

S eason of frost and sunshine, of chill rains and budding trees, of California's mild intermingling with the tempered air of spring—fair season of change and prophecy, when the grass grows fresh up the hillside and the birds are once more inspired to song—I salute thee with reverence and delight!

In February the air is full of expectancy, and nature seems busy with mighty preparations for a new year of toil. The spiders come forth from their hiding-places and run nimbly over the land. The field-mice and wood-rats are at work in their run-ways amid the grass of the hillsides or the underbrush of the cañons [sic]. The ground-squirrels emerge from their tunneled retreats to sport in the open fields. Earth and air are pregnant with new life, soon to be born in all the glory and splendor of spring.

It is at such times that we are most forcibly reminded of the unceasing change that is ever in progress in nature. Each day brings forth something new, year in and year out. At times the transition is more or less rapid or conspicuous, but it never ceases. Like the waters of the ocean with their perpetual ebb and flow, so all that lives has its periods of rise and fall, and February marks the incoming tide of life.

Charles Keeler, in *Bird Notes Afield,* 1899

Charles Keeler was a prolific writer and naturalist who moved to Berkeley in the late 1880s from Wisconsin. He attended the University of California and worked for the California Academy of Sciences, but his main contribution was spreading the architectural principles and influence of his good friend Bernard Maybeck. Keeler was an ardent advocate of the Arts and Crafts movement, which called for handmade simplicity and harmony with nature in architectural and landscape design.

The movement lasted until the twenties, when audacity roared

Standing from left to right: John Muir, William Keith, Charles Keeler. Seated left to right: John Burroughs, Francis Brown (editor of the Chicago Dial*). Taken in 1909 in Keith's Berkeley studio. (PHOTO COURTESY OF BERKELEY ARCHITECTURAL HERITAGE ASSOCIATION)*

past simplicity and Keeler's writings faded into obscurity. Yet anyone, today, who walks the lanes and steps presented here and admires the harmony of house and hill, of garden and path, of town and greenbelt, owes Charles Keeler a thought of thanks.

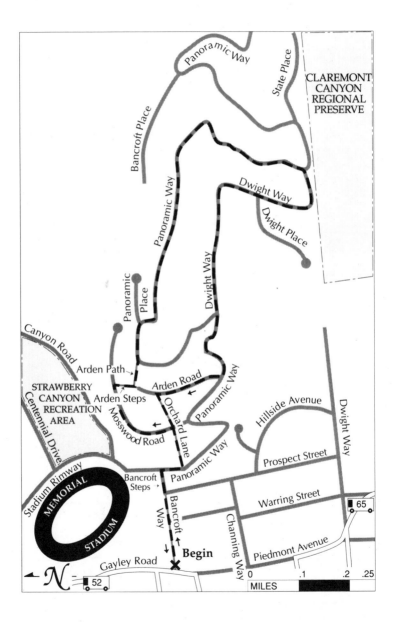

10

A Panoramic Way
& an Orchard Lane

Terrain: *moderate to steep; improved lanes and steps*
Bus lines: *52, 52C*
Parks: *UC Berkeley stadium complex, UC Botanical Gardens*
Shops: *Bancroft Way and Telegraph Avenue area, Euclid Avenue at North Gate of campus*
Distance: *1.9 miles*
Directions: *From University Avenue, go north on Shattuck to Hearst Avenue. Turn right and continue past Euclid Avenue, bearing right onto Gayley Road. This becomes Piedmont Avenue near Bancroft Way and the International House.*

J ust before the turn of the century, this area in the hills south of the UC campus was mostly orchards and horse trails. With the growing numbers of students and faculty, though, the realtors, Mason-McDuffie, saw the housing potential and soon drew up plans to develop the area. In 1910, the firm's Henry Atkins designed the ornate Orchard Lane, named for an almond orchard which previously occupied the site, and, influenced by the Hillside Club and architects like Coxhead, Morgan, and Maybeck, a neighborhood that reflected the style of that era. The streets wind like water looking for the path of least resistance. The houses blend tastefully with the environment.

The paths, steps, and streets favor the walker, as traffic must carefully negotiate the narrow, sharply curved former horse trails like Panoramic Way. And the views, in places, are among the best anywhere in the Bay Area.

The walk starts on Piedmont Avenue and Bancroft Way near the university's International House (its friendly cafe is open to the public). Go east on Bancroft and walk straight, up the steps where Warring Street begins. These busy steps lead to Prospect Street and the university's stadium. Continue straight to the start of Panoramic Way, which winds to the right, and look for the steps and sign for Orchard Lane very soon on the left. Climb past its Grecian revival balustrades and benches to the top, where its pillars show the cracks and stresses of nearly a century of earthquake activity. The intent of this design was to make Berkeley the "Athens of the West," and architecture like this was part of that movement.

You're now on Panoramic again, but before rounding its horseshoe bend, bear left to Mosswood Road and walk up the mild grade past brown-shingled houses and views of the stadium, the Campanile, Strawberry Canyon, and much of Berkeley. Julia Morgan designed #11 in 1928. To the right, opposite #37, the Arden Steps begin, all 101 of them, and carry you (if it were only that easy) to the Arden Path to the left, marked by a sign. These steps and path culminate at a solid wooden stairway up to ubiquitous Panoramic Way once again. Go left, continuing for a short way until you turn left again on a narrow street much more suited to walking than driving. You are now officially in Oakland.

At the top, bear right, still on Panoramic Way as it becomes more like a peaceful footpath than a street. It joins Dwight Way, at the open space area above the former California School for the Deaf (now UC Berkeley's Clark Kerr Campus) where grand views open to Oakland, San Francisco, the Bay Bridge, Mt. Tamalpais —just about everything of visual interest around the bay.

Go right on Dwight Way, past Dwight Place, and continue beyond the Panoramic Way turnoff to Arden Road on the right. Climb aerobically, filling your lungs with that high, (mostly) clean East Bay hills air.

Opposite #62, see Orchard Lane to the left and descend to Panoramic. Carefully, and with much awareness, jag left around the always active and dangerous horseshoe curve, back to the same section of Orchard Lane as the beginning of the walk. Retrace your original steps on Panoramic Way around the corner to Prospect and down the steps back to Bancroft Way and the International House, where you can catch your breath and have a well-earned snack at the cafe.

"A Glimpse of the Birds of Berkeley"

As the seasons come and go, a host of birds tarry within the confines of Berkeley, some to make their nests and rear their broods, others to sojourn for but a brief interval in passing from their summer to their winter haunts, and in the joyful return of spring. They inhabit the spreading branches of the live-oaks, and the open meadows are their home. They dwell in the leafy recesses of the cañons [sic] and haunt the shrubbery of our gardens.

It is impossible to understand our birds without knowing something of their surroundings — of the lovely reach of ascending plain from the bay shore to the rolling slopes of the Berkeley Hills (mountains, our eastern friends call them); of the cold, clear streams of water which have cut their way from the hill crests down into the plain, forming lovely cañons with great old live-oaks in their lower and more open portions, and sweet-scented laurel or bay trees crowded into their narrower and more precipitous parts; of the great expanse of open hill slopes, green and tender during the months of winter rain, and soft brown and purple when the summer sun has parched the grass and flower. These, with cultivated gardens and fields of grain, make the environment of our birds, and here they live their busy lives.

Charles Keeler, in *Bird Notes Afield,* 1899

Oakland

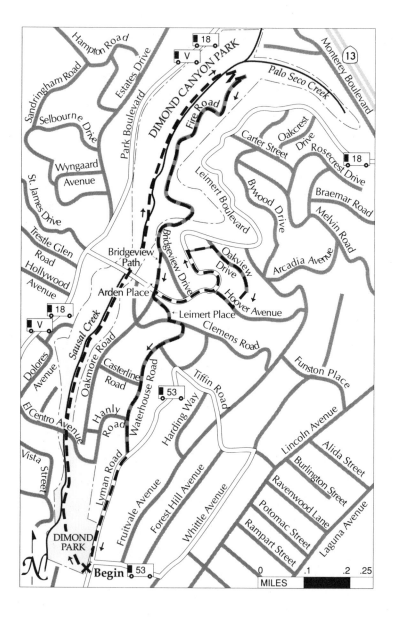

11

Through & Around
Dimond Canyon

Terrain: *easy to steep and rugged; trails, rough creekbed, unimproved paths, improved lanes and steps*

Special Equipment: *hiking shoes with good traction, extra socks in the rainy season*

Bus lines: *53*

Parks: *Dimond Park, Joaquin Miller*

Shops: *Upper Fruitvale Avenue in Dimond District*

Distance: *3.6 miles*

Directions: *From Route 580 (MacArthur Freeway) take the Fruitvale exit, turn left on Fruitvale Avenue, past MacArthur Boulevard to Dimond Park.*

Dimond Park in Oakland sits like a gem on a setting above the MacArthur Freeway that is a different world than below. It is a relatively safe neighborhood with attractive, mostly owner-occupied houses, on winding streets that, like North Berkeley, follow the contours of the hills. The park has tennis and basketball courts, picnic areas, lawns, a playground, a community swimming pool, and some old and noble trees, including the Dimond Oak, about 200 years old and considered to be the oldest oak in Oakland. Next to the tree, in the center of the park, is a house originally built with adobe bricks in 1893 and destroyed by fire in 1953. One adobe wall is still intact and more of its original adobe bricks can be found as part of the retaining wall around the Dimond Oak. Oakland's first mayor and one of its founders, Horace Carpentier, in his initial speech to his city council in April, 1854, talked of his town's "magnificent grove of evergreen oaks," and was passionate about their preservation. "In fact, the destruction of a single tree on whose land soever it stands, should be considered a public injury," he promulgated. "I recommend the passage of an ordinance for the protection of shade trees, under the heaviest penalty authorized by the Charter."

This walk begins on Fruitvale Avenue at the entrance to Dimond Park. As the name Fruitvale implies, this entire area was mostly fruit orchards in the early part of the twentieth century and was considered a country retreat by Bay Area urbanites at that time. Walk up the steps to the park, taking the paved path past old oaks, redwoods, Monterey pines, and past the above-mentioned house and Dimond Oak. Note the commemorative bell and plaque explaining the history of the spot. Bear right, keeping the pool to your right, into the playground area and find a dirt path at the far end.

Two short metal posts mark the trail's beginning, with Sausal Creek (dry in summer at this section) to your left. At El Centro Avenue, cross at the crosswalk to the left to the start of the Dimond Canyon Hiking Trail, which was blazed by the city of Oakland in conjunction with the East Bay Regional Park District. With the exception of some WPA flood control projects in the late thirties, Sausal Creek and its canyon are as wild as they ever were. There are mostly California native plants and trees throughout, with steep canyon walls separating you from the rest of Oakland's 350,000 people. A large wooden sign and map are posted at the trailhead.

The trail starts out wide and woodsy following the increasingly water-filled creek. After a while, though, you'll need to scramble over some of those WPA concrete reinforcements. The Works Project Administration was definitely walker-friendly, as you can see from the stepping stones and drain cover over a section funneling runoff water from the top of the canyon. The federal agency was responsible for building a number of the pathways and parks featured in this book.

Beyond the culvert, it looks like the trail ends and, in a sense, it does. It's here that the creekbed doubles as a trail with the bank above occasionally usable. The canyon is steeper here and the air damper. There are more bay laurel trees growing thick and wild.

You'll need to go slower here, finding just the right stepping stones to make your way up the creek. The slower pace gives you a better chance to smell the laurel or watch the spindly water walkers where the creek collects in pools. It gives you time to open to feelings waiting for wildness to set them free.

Next are a series of small falls created by the WPA, probably to slow the rush of water in the rainy season, and a small tunnel culvert ahead. Follow the cool, shady dirt trail to the left of the tunnel. The creek is underground here but soon surfaces again with the trail continuing to the left. Shortly, you're back at the creekbed needing to ford the stream to the other side where a signpost, "Dimond Canyon Trail," points the way up and out of the canyon.

Take this route if the creek is fairly dry and stepping stones are available. But after a few winter storms, you may need to backtrack about 25 feet, finding a narrow trail that takes you above and a little farther up the creek. Here, at another waterfall, next to a substantial stone retaining wall, it may be easier to cross. The sign here points right, to the same way out of the canyon as before.

The trail snakes upward, made easier by a series of switchbacks up the wild and deep canyon. There's more live oak now as the environment becomes drier. The California live oak is an evergreen, unlike other deciduous species of oak in other parts of the country.

At the top is a wider and level dirt fire road. A left will take you to Monterey Boulevard, the public Montclair Golf Course, and eventually to trails leading to Joaquin Miller Park in the hills above Oakland. It's an option if you've arranged a car shuttle or want to try to return by public transportation. But a right on the fire road will be a much more convenient loop route.

Follow the road to Bridgeview Drive as the sky opens and views of the hills south of San Francisco appear. At another signpost pointing vaguely to Bridgeview Drive, bear right (do not go straight) around the bend (notice the rustic hillside redwood house above) and through the gateway onto Bridgeview.

Descend Bridgeview Path (admiring the red-tiled roofs along the way), marked by a sign on the right and just before #4341, to Arden Place. Turn left, finding Leimert Boulevard and a small commercial area with a food market. Go left on Leimert bending past Hoover, to the steps on the right just after #1735 (a telephone pole also marks the spot). Climb the asphalt and railroad tie steps to Oakview Drive. A right brings you to the end of this cul-de-sac and a set of more improved concrete steps, with an iron railing, to the right. These were built by the WPA in 1939 when this section was developing. Along the way notice cedar, laurel, and views of Oakland and the bay.

At the bottom is Hoover, where a right-of-way for another section of the path exists but perhaps the WPA ran out of money. A right takes you to Leimert, where you turn sharply to the left onto Leimert Place. Views of the towering Mormon Temple open as you bear right onto Waterhouse Road (after passing Clemens Road). Continue on this winding street, always bearing left where other streets enter. Notice #4036 with its stained glass, whimsical klinker brick chimney, and unusual roof lines. The cedar shingle roof of #3853, too, is a piece of the architecture of an earlier, less hurried time.

Waterhouse joins Lyman Road near the bottom of the hill and Dimond Park, with all its amenities and old-growth trees, reappears on the right. While in the depths of Dimond Canyon, you may have wondered if you'd ever get back, but here you are.

Wildness: The Hills

*T*o walk in wild places is good for the urban dweller. The free wind, the swaying grasses and trees, the music of birds, the squish of mud are things easily forgotten as we rush about our daily routines. The drone of accumulation can deaden the spirit, so visiting a place where no consuming occurs is rejuvenating.

And the East Bay is fortunate that wise people had the foresight, sensitivity, and courage, during the Great Depression, to set up a regional park system that made a portion of the hills wild forever. Otherwise that whole expanse of parkland would now be neighborhoods.

These hills help quiet the mind. They are innocent and alive, unconcerned with getting something or somewhere, no interest in gaining position, power or status, having nothing to do with image or sex appeal or political persuasion. Beings are born there without great celebration and beings die there without remorse. Beings receive and give there without judgement. Living things there do not need to work on getting balanced or centered. Their core is in balance.

The pace of life is slow there, in this place that has no pace at all—a place that, without the labels of geology, would be of no time, no sense of past, present or future. To walk in a timeless place must at some level make us whole, and resonate with that part of us which is perfectly at ease.

Tilden Park, at least part of it, is such a place. It is a magnanimous world that announces with a fresh breeze, "Welcome, walk here in peace." The Tilden hills above Berkeley have never turned me away. Nor do they beckon. They are simply there, expecting nothing, giving everything.

I remember a late afternoon in winter when there was mud and fog—a penetrating fog that obscured all outward views but opened up inner ones. It was simply a walk in the fog in a wild place. Even the Self involved in the walking was minimized, for in dense fog, in a place where there are no houses, cars, or stores, there are fewer reference points to stir the memory of "me." In fact there were no longer any memories of this familiar Big Springs trail, for the fog erased them. The fog made it much less possible to name what was seen, and so without the mental activity of naming there was a direct relationship, a direct connection with the wild hills.

And with that connection, the essence of the hills and the walker of hills were revealed. Something unnameable. Something without time. Something wild, untamed, yet completely disciplined and in order. To be in such communion with one's environment is healing — more healing than any human contrivance or word. For it has little to do with the will. It comes uninvited, gently.

These hills do not want or seek. There is no looking forward to or looking back at. There is no making changes. Changes just happen. There is no wishing the bad ones away or hoping for the good ones. There is only the activity of innocence, of sensitivity, and with innocence and sensitivity, ironically, come maturity.

Being mature, the wild hills of the East Bay are a trusting place, completely open and vulnerable, receptive to all, resisting none. And without resistance or expectation, the heart opens. It is a moment of change and communion. No fear. No doubt. No analyzing or processing. No you or I.

The hills are covered with misty morning light now. There is a spirit there that calls to all spirits to stop for a moment and look — and in the Bay Area that can be from just about anywhere. To notice them in the middle of a busy day settles the mind in a way no thought or word can.

At this moment, the hills feel as friends. Their soft contours convey an ease, with life, with change. The wildness within the hills is firmly rooted, forever offering respite and good company.

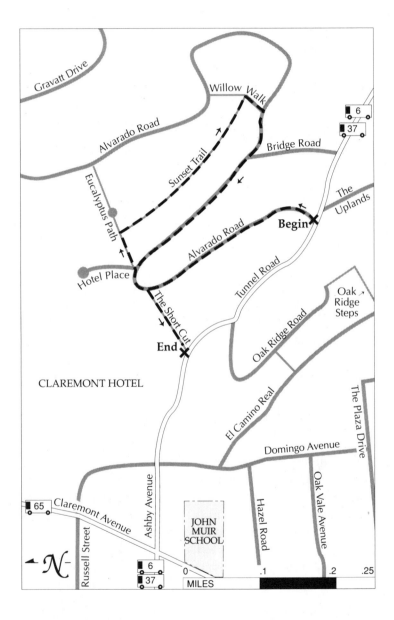

12

The Alvarado Loop
&
The Short Cut

Terrain: *easy to moderate; improved paths and steps, unimproved trail*
Bus Lines: *65, 6, or 37*
Parks: *John Muir School playground on Claremont Avenue near Ashby*
Shops: *Domingo Street off Tunnel Road*
Distance: *1 mile*
Directions: *Take Ashby Avenue heading east, past College Avenue, past Claremont, to a left onto Alvarado Road.*

The Claremont Hotel, on the border between Berkeley and Oakland, has been an East Bay institution since the early days of this century. Soon after it was built, the all-electric Key System, a trolley line, was extended there, opening the area to residential development. To compensate for the hilly terrain, planners came up with Alvarado Road, a snake of a road that winds through the older, established neighborhood above the hotel. Out of probable compassion to walkers, along with aesthetics, they included several interesting short-cuts as well.

Start this walk on Alvarado, which is off Tunnel Road, just within Oakland's boundary above the Claremont Hotel. Where Alvarado makes the first horseshoe bend to the right see the steep steps of the Eucalyptus Path on the eastern side of the street. This is a long path which, if you went all the way, would take you past a grove of eucalyptus, large gardens, and eventually to Alvarado, providing a shortcut to the winding street. But a better route is to take the Sunset Trail, which enters about a third of the way up the Eucalyptus Path.

The trail itself is unmarked at this point but look for a city lamppost and a small eucalyptus grove. Take the level dirt path to the right and enjoy the south of San Francisco bay views and sunset, if it's that time of day. This leads to an old signpost and the junction with the Willow Walk. To the left, the Willow Walk leads up to Alvarado, which is where you would have eventually gone had you taken the Eucalyptus Walk to the top.

It's a quiet spot that feels right out of Hansel and Gretel's forest, sequestered by great redwoods and pines. Go right on the Willow Walk to, again, Alvarado and continue to the right, a quiet refuge from the tumultuous traffic of Tunnel Road. This brings you back to the start, but before you leave, look to the left and see a path that leads down to the Claremont Hotel parking lot. This is The Short Cut, where during the rainy season, you can sit on the stone bench just in from Alvarado and hear Harwood Creek as it flows underground.

Now you have a walker's choice of descending The Short Cut, checking out the well-equipped playground at the John Muir School near the corner of Claremont and Ashby (if you have kids along), browsing in the mini-gourmet ghetto on Domingo, reviewing the Claremont Hotel's impressive 20-acre garden, and/or returning up The Short Cut.

The Claremont Hotel: Romanticism Retained

*T*hree things shaped the birth and prosperity of the Bay Area's only resort hotel: the Gold Rush, a checker game, and a UC Berkeley coed.

When Bill Thornberg, a Kansas farmer, struck it rich in the gold fields, he promised his wife a home that would look like an English castle. So he bought 13,000 acres from the original Spanish land grant and built her just that: a castle with stables of pedigreed horses and Cockney grooms to attend to them, and even English foxes, raised for hunting parties. Unlike Dorothy in the land of Oz, it seems as if Bill forgot about Kansas pretty quickly.

When his wife died and his daughter moved to England to marry a British lord, he sold the place, and not a moment too soon. In July, 1901, it burned to the ground leaving only the stables and a barn (which became locker rooms for the hotel's pool and tennis club).

The property then transferred to three East Bay tycoons who planned a resort hotel with trains running straight into the lobby. But when plans bogged down, they had a checker game, in the old Athenian Club of Oakland, with the stakes being the land where the hotel was to sit. Attorney Frank Havens won, beating out Francis "Borax" Smith, the Death Valley borax miner who put his wealth into linking real estate development with public transportation. In fact, after the Claremont Hotel was completed in 1915, just in time for the Panama Pacific Exposition in San Francisco, Smith, never missing an opportunity, extended his Key Route electric train system up Claremont Avenue, to service the hotel's guests.

Due to financial problems, it took nine years to complete the Mediterranean-style Claremont, but once finished, it flourished,

The Key System train, Claremont Avenue, the Claremont Hotel, St. John's Episcopal Church, the Claremont Park entrance gates, and the area included in the Alvarado Loop Walk as they appeared around 1912. (PHOTO COURTESY BERKELEY HISTORICAL SOCIETY)

until a quirky state law crimped the profits. It was the same 1873 edict, now resurrected, that prohibited the sale of alcohol within a mile radius of the University of California. The authorities assumed the hotel was inside that dry mile, and in 1936, the Claremont was one of the few hotels in the Bay Area which did not have a bar.

But a UC Berkeley student, who wished the situation were different, began her own investigation of the hotel's proximity to the college. With a group of friends, she stepped off the shortest distance between the campus and the hotel's front porch. It was more than a mile by just a few feet and a bar was born—the present Terrace Bar. And the woman? The temperance movement would definitely have not called it a reward, but she was given free drinks at the bar for the rest of her life.

Since then the hotel, straddling the Berkeley-Oakland border, has been renovated extensively, but its white balconies and towers and manicured 20-acre garden are still reminders of the Age of Romanticism that inspired its design.

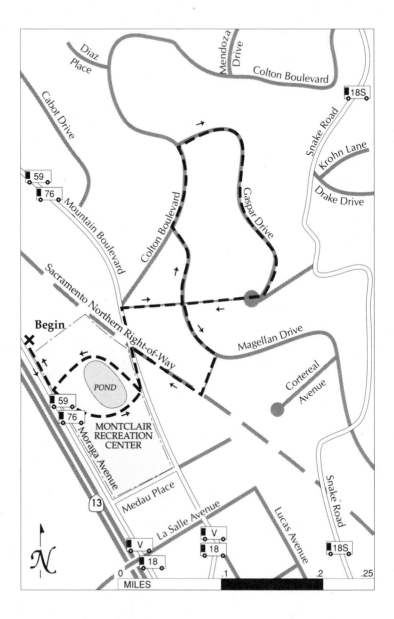

13

Montclair Ways

Terrain: *easy to steep; improved steps, unimproved trails*
Bus lines: *59, 76, 18*
Special Equipment: *shoes with good traction, and/or a walking stick*
Parks: *Montclair Recreation Center*
Shops: *Montclair Village along Mountain Boulevard*
Distance: *1.5 miles*
Directions: *Take Montclair District exit off Route 13 (Warren Freeway), following Moraga Boulevard to fire station and Recreation Center.*

If you didn't know the area and drove through Montclair, you'd probably think it was a separate town. It has that feel about it: a sense of community, an identity apart from Oakland, which it is actually a part of. In fact there are some in town who would like to see it do just that: split off from Oakland and have its own government. But the Oakland City Council might take to the trenches before it lets such a jewel get away. Not only would it lose substantial tax revenues from Montclair's expensive houses and affluent residents but it would also lose its mountain-like village in the hills.

Start this walk on Moraga Avenue, the street adjacent to the Warren Freeway, at the fire station — perhaps the most architecturally interesting fire station in the Bay Area. According to the chief, who is also the department's historian, the station was built in 1927 and was designed to look like a mountain chalet. It was always meant to be a fire station, but there were also plans, which never materialized, to use it as a community hall. It's right on the Hayward Fault, but the chief said the building is sound and has held up well over the years. You're welcome to go in and look around. Just ask for the chief.

Proceed past the tennis courts to the entrance of the Montclair Recreation Center, which may also be one of the most unusual of its kind in the area. Entering, see the start of an exercise "Gamefield," a mock-western play town on the right, and a nicely designed pond on the left, with its resident ducks and geese. There are also wooden jungle gyms, a ball field, basketball courts, more tennis courts, sandboxes, redwood trees, and the community center building itself.

If you can get anyone in your party to leave, take the stone steps between the pond and the tennis courts up to Mountain Boulevard and turn left. Walk to the first crosswalk, which is next to Colton Boulevard, cross, and climb the steep, well-made concrete steps, which have neither sign nor name, at the corner. This brings you to Magellan Drive, where you turn left. Go to Colton, bear right, and descend a short way — walk this few hundred feet carefully as the street is winding and busy and has no sidewalks — to Gaspar Drive. Walk up steeply to the right, past towering redwood homes with decks and abundant flower boxes. There's an undeveloped hillside to the left with graceful pampas grass, tenacious scotch broom, young oaks and pines, and, of course, the ubiquitous eucalyptus.

At the top, to the right, see a driveway just past #1951. Between the line of pines beyond the driveway and #1961, find concrete steps with an iron railing on the right side. Like many of the hidden paths in this book, it looks private but isn't. The unmarked lane drops between tall eucalyptus trees to the right and a house immediately to the left. The view quickly opens to the Oakland hills and the freeway as the pathway and steps channel you to Magellan.

Now turn left to just past #1875 and opposite #1878 to a path you'd think would get you locked up for using. It's an unmarked dirt trail, next to a telephone pole, that slips down to the right past a house on the left and a small wire fence farther down on the right. "Slips" is the right word, as pine needles and eucalyptus buds make the trek a precarious one. Railroad ties near the top help, but down near the fence there's nothing to cling to except caution. Just concentrate on your footing all the way down and you should be fine.

The path rockets you onto an asphalt right-of-way once used by the Sacramento Northern Railway to take passengers as far as Sacramento and Chico. Go right, seeing the downtown shopping area below, and then straight on the dirt path before the improved path turns towards downtown. Shortly, come to concrete steps and a red iron railing leading down to Mountain Boulevard. A right brings you to the same crosswalk at Colton, where you then retrace your steps back into the Recreation Center park (which is closed between 10 P.M. and 6 A.M., in case you're a late night walker).

At the pond, follow its bank and path, this time, to the right, crossing lava stepping stones under very willowy willows that droop into the pond. Bear left around the pond, and return (or stay and play for awhile) through the gate to Moraga and the fanciful fire chalet.

Joaquin Miller

*H*is real name was Cincinnatus Heiner Miller, but he took the name Joaquin because it more fit the image he was trying to convey. He called himself "The Poet of the Sierras" and was widely regarded in European literary circles. Often traveling to London, he attended lavish parties attired in sombrero, cowhide boots, and red shirt, open at the collar. When asked about this, he replied, "It helps sell the poems, boys, and it tickles the duchesses."

He had been a Confederate sympathizer in a state that was free, but on his death in 1913, his huge estate in the hills was willed to his beloved Oakland. The city accepted the donation and named it Joaquin Miller Park in his honor.

His romantic poetry has survived neither the test of time nor critics, but he does convey a feeling for Oakland that would warm the heart of any present-day booster.

Oakland

Thou Rose-Land! Oakland! thou mine own!
Thou Sun-land! Leaf-land! Land of seas
Wide crescented in walls of stone!
Thy lion's mane is to the breeze!
Thy tawney [sic], sunlit lion steeps
Leap forward as the lion leaps!
And thou, the lion's whelp begot
Of Argonauts, in fearful strength
And supple beauty yieldeth naught!
Thine arm is as a river's length.
Thy reach is foremost! Thou shalt be
The throned queen of this vast, west sea!
Yet here sits peace; and rest sits here,
These wide-boughed [sic] oaks, they house wise men;
The student and the sage austere;

The men of wonderous [sic] thought and ken.
Here men of God in holy guise
Invoke the peace of Paradise.
Be this my home till some fair star
Stoops earthward and shall beckon me;
For surely God-land lies not far
From these Greek heights and this great sea.
My friend, my love, trend this way;
Not far along lies Arcady.

Joaquin Miller

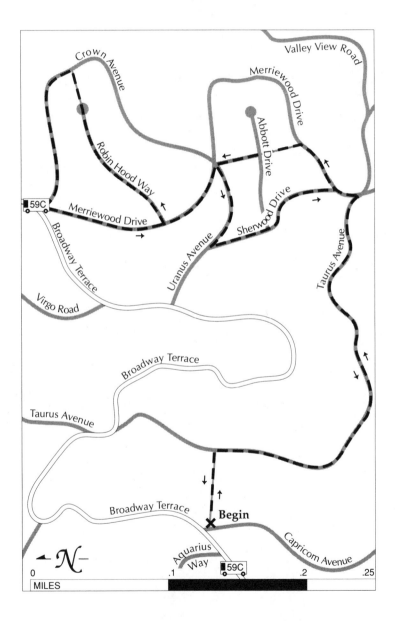

14

Higher Montclair Ways

Terrain: *easy to steep; improved steps and lanes, unimproved paths and steps*
Bus lines: *59C from Moraga Avenue in the village*
Parks: *Montclair Recreation Center*
Shops: *Montclair Village*
Distance: *1.8 miles*
Directions: *From Mountain Boulevard in the village head west to Broadway Terrace. Turn right and proceed to the junction with Capricorn Avenue.*

The origins of Montclair village go back to the 1850s, when Colonel Jack Hayes, who turned out to be the East Bay's first realtor, bought part of the huge Peralta ranchero and chose a spot near the present Moraga Avenue and Thornhill Drive for his home. In fact, Moraga was originally called Jack Hayes Canyon Road, after he created a wagon road up the ravine. He and his friend John Fremont, the first American to extensively explore California, would look out at the sunset over the bay from Hayes' house, inspiring Fremont to name the narrow strait before them the "Golden Gate."

A large dairy farm followed Hayes, the eastern part of which eventually became Montclair village and the rest evolving into part of present-day Piedmont. In the early 1900s, the Sacramento Northern Railroad began running passenger trains from Fortieth and Shafter streets in Oakland through Montclair and on to Sacramento and Chico. And a few years later, in the early twenties, the first subdivision opened in Montclair. According to real estate advertisements at the time, the area was "regarded as the ideal place to live, nestled among oak, eucalyptus, Monterey pine and cypress trees."

At first, though, the only buyers were San Franciscans wanting vacation homes. They'd take the ferry, then the Key system train to Piedmont, then a day-long horse and buggy ride to get into the steep hills where this walk is. Most of the development has been in the last 25 years and residents are no longer just vacationers.

Start this walk where Broadway Terrace and Capricorn Avenue intersect, just past Aquarius Avenue. Wooden steps, at the beginning of Capricorn, lie between the redwood deck of the house on the right and the cyclone fence of the unusual house on the left. This house, built as a speculative venture by a developer and a graft between Mediterranean and Southwest styles, is disliked by some neighbors who would have preferred unpainted redwood. It is unoccupied at this writing.

But even redwood doesn't always please, as the controversy surrounding the redwood deck to the right demonstrates. It seems the builder was about to usurp the right-of-way that made the steps and path possible, causing neighbors to organize, appeal to the city, and save the path. Their winning argument was that the right-of-way was an important fire escape for those living in the hills above.

The wooden steps lead to crude steps created with railroad ties which lead to an even rougher path next to the cyclone fence up to Taurus Avenue. Turn right and continue on Taurus past the quiet garden at #65, brick and redwood houses and cottages tucked above and below, and bay views as you walk higher. The lazy street is more like a mountain trail as it winds along the hills, finally joining a five-corner intersection.

Veer sharply to the left onto Sherwood Drive — unsigned as of this writing — then a right at the first street on the right, Merriewood Drive. Locals call this section Sherwood Forest for its street name references to Robin Hood.

After about 200 feet, climb the wooden steps to the left, next to #5921. There's a green and white fire hydrant and a huge Monterey pine to mark the spot. The ill-defined path above skirts a fence on the left, goes under an apple tree, and then continues, now paved, past Abbott Drive to a four-corner intersection. Take Merriewood to the left (not nearby Uranus Avenue), going past the brick home on the right to a right at Robin Hood Way. The sign says it's not a through street, but that applies only to cars.

At the end of this dead-end street (which would be a good one for Robin and his merry band to live on), take the dirt path to the right between two large pines and follow it down and to the left, stepping carefully over some natural pine- root steps onto Crown Avenue. Make sure the Sheriff of Nottingham is not in sight and go left around the bend, with views of wilder, mostly undeveloped hills to the north.

At the four corners, turn left on Merriewood, past another tucked away cottage at #6222 — suitable for Little John — to a right on Uranus at the bottom of the hill. A left on Sherwood takes you past Abbott, where a short diversion is in order to see the house at #1, a symphony of brick, wood, shingle and stained glass that would certainly be Robin and Marion's headquarters.

Return to Sherwood and turn right onto Taurus at the five corners. You're on the same street as before but in a westerly direction this time. Just past #65, next to a phone pole, carefully descend the controversial path and right of way you started with, back to Broadway Terrace and Capricorn. Maybe the spirit of Robin Hood helped save it.

The Hi-Line

*T*here is a simple, though worldly, phenomenon that occurs when taking walks in wilder places. It is not an event that will make the evening news. Nor is it something to rush home and report about. But the moment it happens, there is a universal alignment that immediately affects life on earth. It is a place where people pass and say hello. It is the "Hi-Line."

The Hi-Line is always out and away from congestion, and from automobiles in particular. It is often higher than nearby towns or cities, but not necessarily: you can cross the Hi-Line at sea level, within parks at the outskirts of cities and on meandering back roads trickling into small, lazy towns. It is usually near nature, and it's always under some vast quantity of sky, regardless of that sky's condition. You can find the Hi-Line in a drizzle as well as a drought.

Now within the craw of cities there does exist an "eye-line" where passersby (and sometimes driversby) glance at each other; but to raise the white flag and say "hi" would arouse distrust to the point of malice. A grunt, with the decibels of a burp, is about all that greets such open gestures, as the startled grunter grumbles away. But in more remote places, there is less suspicion so a simple greeting is just a simple greeting.

Yet a "hi" is not automatic. There are several factors and conditions that play into it. Whereas one-on-one meetings invariably result in some form of salutation, when one person meets two, particularly on paths near cities, the chances of a "hi" tapers off. This is not true in backcountry areas where any numbers of people will always exchange greetings. But near cities, the two companions are often so deep in conversation, they don't even look up. The talk is often intense, animated, and serious, allowing little space for a glance much less a "hi." If one of the talkers should look up and note the passerby, he or she might utter something like a "hi," but it's a loath sound much like the aforementioned eye-line grunt.

Now if the solitary walker meets a group of three or more, there is often significant "hi" activity. The talk is more superficial so all it takes is one in the group to look up, acknowledge the fellow walker and "hi." At this cue, most of the others "hi," with the exception of a consistent few who make it a point never to "hi," although even these iconoclasts usually can't resist at least a smile.

An even more engaging situation arises out of two-on-two configurations, particularly when there are romantic involvements within both parties. At times, if the talk is solemn, the couples might pass each other like commuters in a train station. But more often what happens is a tacit acknowledgement of relationships in progress — acknowledgement of risk taking. So conversations stop for a moment and everyone greets each other respectfully. There's a camaraderie, however brief.

The Hi-Line transcends distance, aloofness, and anomie, giving us entry into other lives. The sound of the human voice, friendly and open, is healing, adding harmony to this dissonant world. You don't have to qualify for a "hi" at the Hi-Line. No applications to fill out. Nobody's asking what you do or where you live or who you vote for. There's less judging going on.

Maybe it's the spaciousness. There's more room to breathe. The air is fresher and more vital; and so are the people. In the congested places, the game is to avoid bumping into objects and people, not easy given the density. We walk or drive around with blinders, training ourselves to attend only to the task in front — sometimes days in front — of us. We don't see each other except to avoid collision (and, given the statistics, don't do all that well with that either).

But in places less touched by technology and commerce, human contact is replenished. Clots dissolve in an environment that nurtures friendliness. Good will and trust rule the ridges.

Of course, anyone, anywhere could draw the Hi-Line. All you need to do is say "hi" to a passerby. It's risky. There may be rejection or, worse, no response at all. But, on the other hand, the stranger might smile back and reciprocate with a "Hi, how ya doin'." (Peripatetic studies have shown one-on-one conditions give the highest "hi" probabilities.)

When you think how few people in the world exchange friendly words with us, the Hi-Line is an important place to frequent. It's a place where old, familiar souls can meet, in passing, and reassure each other of their inherent affability.

Piedmont

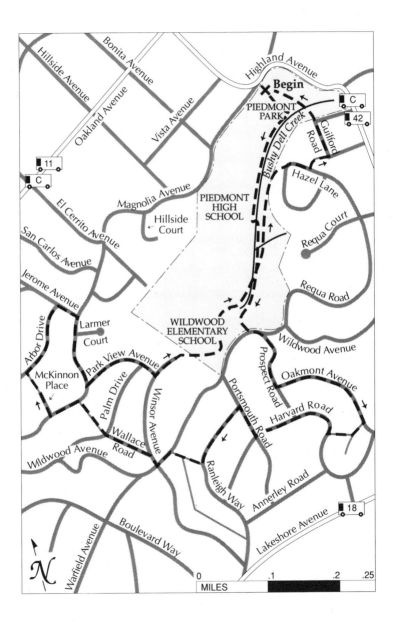

15

Anonymous Paths & a Wild Park

Terrain: *easy to moderate; unimproved lanes and trails, improved paths and steps in varying conditions.*
Bus line: *Piedmont "C" from Fortieth and MacArthur BART*
Parks: *Piedmont Park, Oakland's Rose Garden off Grand, Wildwood Elementary School playground*
Shops: *Grand and Lakeshore Avenues in Oakland*
Distance: *3.4 miles*
Directions: *From 580, take Oakland Avenue exit and follow past Grand Avenue to Highland Avenue in Piedmont. Turn right to center of town and Piedmont Park a few blocks away.*

iedmont's first house was a modest one, built in 1862. Ten years before, Walter Blair, a dairy farmer from Vermont, had bought 600 acres of what was to become a major part of the town of Piedmont for $1.60 an acre. Since then, the houses have become more ornate and the land slightly more expensive, making this one of the Bay Area's most exclusive places to live. From its bucolic origins, Piedmont was "discovered" after two white sulphur springs attracted the attention of speculators who saw the possibilities of a resort hotel on the site. A horse-car line was extended from Piedmont Avenue, and the Piedmont Hotel was built in 1876 at the springs in what is now Piedmont Park. It thrived into the 1880s but degenerated into a rowdy saloon, until fire finally destroyed it in 1886. "Small wonder each householder kept a loaded revolver handy," wrote a local historian, "and carried it with him on any lonely night drives."

This walk starts in a much safer Piedmont Park, a 28-acre gem in the center of town on Highland Avenue south of Oakland Avenue. Mark Twain visited the sulphur springs on these grounds in 1867. You can enter these same grounds in several places, but the Grecian archway, with its delicate turquoise urn in the center, at Magnolia and Highland avenues, across from the police station, is the most elegant. Just beyond the entrance is one of several unusual, turn-of-the-century concrete benches, crafted with steel and cement.

Take the path to the left of the bench and descend through the redwoods to Bushy Dell Creek. Follow the path to the left of the creek, which flows year round, to a set of concrete steps with black iron rails. Walk down and go left through the wooded path past a waterfall near three large eucalyptus trees. The eucalyptus was a valued tree when the hotel was thriving, and one huge specimen graced the entrance to the park until street paving choked off its water supply.

The wooded path continues to the left of the creek, past small waterfalls, horsetails, cedar, coast live oak, pine, laurel, maple, and a natural eucalyptus-root bridge, that looks like rustic, late-nineteenth-century carpentry. A little further, the creek rushes through a finely crafted stone culvert, before it goes underground just before a playground. Stay left on the dirt path rising above the playground and onto Wildwood Avenue. Bear left on Wildwood, then make a quick right onto Prospect Road where the playful klinker brick chimney at #25 appears.

At Oakmont Avenue go left and then right at an unmarked alley just after #98. Entering this small lane, see a narrow path to the right, next to a metal post and sewer grate. Take the path and steps, which is opposite #106, down to the wide open spaces of Harvard Road. Go right, past Prospect, then right again on Portsmouth Road. This is a newer section of Piedmont, developed in the last 40 years, much different than the opulent mansions higher up (which you'll see in the "Piedmont Hi-Lines" walk).

Turn left on Portsmouth, followed by an immediate right onto Ranleigh Way. At the point where Ranleigh bends to the left take the unmarked and unnamed concrete steps to the right at #1101. This is easy to miss, but if you keep the graceful birch tree to your left, you're on the correct pathway. Climb gently to Wild-wood Avenue, where you turn left. Then go right on Winsor Avenue, where you quickly bear left onto Wallace Road. This short street leads to Palm Drive (a look to either side will reveal how the street got its name). Take the footpath to the left of #201 Palm, first a level grade then up to steps and out onto Magnolia Avenue.

A left here then a quick right at the cul-de-sac, MacKinnon Place, brings you to more steps at the far end. Descend to Arbor Drive then go right, up past the attractive cut-stone house at #135, a welcome relief from the surrounding stucco dwellings. Rights on Jerome Avenue and Magnolia, and a left on Park View Avenue where you continue past Palm, bring you to Winsor again. Turning left, see the concrete steps with iron railing at the end of the street to the right of the entrance to a ball field. Take these steps, next to the magnanimous palm, to the grounds of Wildwood Elementary School.

Go left at the top of the steps to a ramp to your left, where you descend until you're even with the goal posts on the field. Walk up the stone steps to the right and then left on a part-dirt, part-concrete trail at the top. This leads past the playground on your left and back into Piedmont Park. Look for the old laurel tree with the hollow base, at this juncture, that will take you or your children right into Wonderland if you let it.

Bear right where the trail soon branches to the right and climb

the canyon of Bushy Dell Creek. Go up steps and then over a tributary creek and bridge with handrails to where the path levels. Continue past two old oaks, their trunks crossed like sentry guards, as you walk high above the creek. The eucalyptus trees still tower above, giving a better view of the height of these giants planted in the last century.

Keep bearing right where the trail branches, adjacent to the large houses above. Take the first asphalt path to the right, next to one of the large buildings, on a lane that improves as it approaches steps that exit onto Hazel Lane. Bear left on this horseshoe street and watch carefully for a set of steps with an iron rail in the center, located to the left of #108. A redwood tree to the right confirms the identification.

The steps and path look private but, in fact, are public, bringing you to a red brick path leading to Guilford Road, where the houses begin to take on that neoclassic, Great Gatsby look. Turn left and in no time you're back in Piedmont Park next to the Japanese tea house and redwood grove. The house, along with the Piedmont Community Hall ahead, can be rented, and often is, for weddings and meetings. At this writing, the pond next the tea house is dry, but word is that it will be filled sometime in the future, as it once was.

You can still stand on its wooden walkways, though, and imagine swapping jokes with Mark Twain.

The Bay Area's First
Brown-Shingled House

Joseph Worcester, a Swedenborgian minister, left Boston in 1869 to settle in the hills east of San Francisco Bay and brought with him architectural ideas that were sprouting on the East Coast. Although not trained as an architect, Rev. Worcester designed his first house, in the Piedmont area, in a low, compact, simple style, much different from the ornate and spacious interiors of the day. He used undecorated, unpainted planks inside and wood shingles on the outside of this cottage that was to become a prototype of a style unique to the Bay Area. Later he built a church of similar design, and when he hired a design firm to assist, one of the draftsmen assigned to the project was Bernard Maybeck.

"The little house, though rough, is attractive and in harmony with the magnificence of view around it," Rev. Worcester wrote to a family member shortly after moving in January, 1878. "Friends will be glad to come to it for relief from city life, and it ought to be a good place for some sober thinking on my part."

And a year later, he wrote to another New England relative, "And now I can say that I never saw more favorable conditions than those that my little house affords. The broad outlook, the modest homely appearance of the house, and the big wooden room with its quiet tone of color; friends say that it is restful. I have been setting out vines about the house this week, climbing roses, passion-vines, begonias, etc. and at a little distance I have set out currant and gooseberry bushes and apple, pear, and cherry trees."

Jack London later rented the house and was equally enchanted by its ambience. "Am beautifully located in new house," he wrote to a friend in 1902. "We have a big living room, every inch of it, floor and ceiling, finished in redwood. We could put the floor space of almost four cottages into this one living room alone. The rest of the house is finished in redwood too, and is very, very comfortable. . . . A most famous porch, broad and long and cool, a big clump of magnificent pines, flowers and flowers galore . . . half of ground in bearing orchard and half sprinkled with California poppies . . . our nearest neighbor is a block away (and there isn't a vacant lot within a mile) our view commands all of San Francisco Bay for a sweep of thirty or forty miles, and all the opposing shores."

But it was when Bernard Maybeck, living in a nearby cottage shortly after he came to California, strolled over to look at the interesting low, shingled house, that the seeds of a San Francisco Bay Tradition style of architecture were planted. "There came to Mr. Maybeck in his early California days an experience that profoundly affected his whole artistic outlook," wrote Charles Keeler of his friend. "He found a cottage in Piedmont on the hills back of Oakland, and next to him the Reverend Joseph Worcester had a little summer retreat. Looking into Mr. Worcester's windows, he saw the interior of the cottage was all of unpainted redwood boards. It was a revelation."

Although remodeled and looking much different than the original, Joseph Worcester's historic house still stands at 575 Blair Avenue in Piedmont.

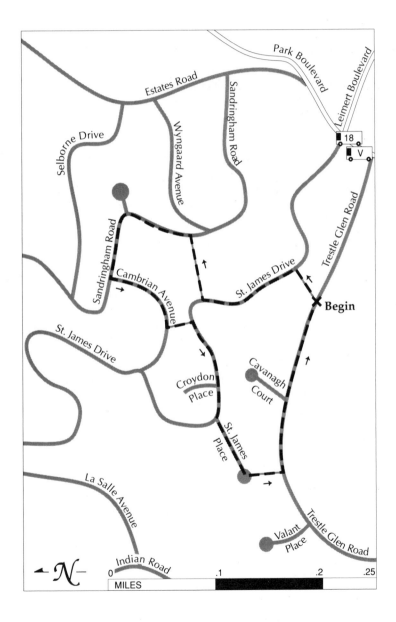

16
Steps of Style

Terrain: *moderate to steep; improved and decorative concrete lanes and steps*
Bus lines: 57 *(From MacArthur BART) to 18*
Parks: *Piedmont Park, Joaquin Miller*
Shops: *Glenview section of Oakland on Park Boulevard*
Distance: *1 mile*
Directions: *From 580, take Park Boulevard exit and go east, turning left on Trestle Glen Avenue, just past the Glenview commercial district.*

In the earlier part of this century, real estate developers were, like those today, out to make a profit. But the earlier entrepreneurs in the Bay Area did it with much more style. This Piedmont neighborhood, known as St. James Wood, just north of Trestle Glen Road was obviously designed by people who not only laid out streets, sidewalks, lanes, and steps, but savored them. They built houses with character, too, and positioned them for views, privacy, slow traffic, and California sunshine.

Start on Trestle Glen Avenue at the steps next to #1822 by a concrete lamppost. Red tiles decorate the steps and can be seen throughout the neighborhood's sidewalks and paths. Go left on St. James Drive at the top.

Unfortunately, the elegant tiled sidewalks on this stylish street are being cracked by the spreading roots of liquidambar trees.

The city has chosen an unstylish asphalt to repair the cracks, leaving the pavement functional but scarred in places.

Continuing, notice the 60-year-old house and Japanese garden at #288. The carved, arched front gate, known as a *torii* gate, is meant by the Japanese to be the only place the Phoenix, the mythical bird that represents immortality, can perch. The large pagoda to the right of the gate was originally a gift from the Japanese emperor to the city of San Francisco for the 1915 Panama-Pacific Exposition.

Proceed on St. James, round a slight bend, then go steeply up the steps to the right just past #254 at another lamppost. This brings you to Sandringham Road and Wyngaard Avenue.

Turn left on Sandringham then left again on Cambrian Avenue, opening to views of the South Bay, red tile, Spanish mission roofs, and Tudor Revival homes. Past #77, go left on the path and steps leading down to St. James Drive. A right at the bottom leads you to St. James Place, not a through street to cars or horse drawn wagons, but walkers can take the red-tiled steps past #60, a handsome Tudor. Descend the steep concrete steps, past ivy and rhododendron, back to Trestle Glen where a left brings you home — a walk that exchanges distance for refinement.

The Key Route &
"Borax" Smith

The story of the Key Route transportation system, an efficient network of ferry and rail service in the Bay Area that operated from the turn of the century to the late fifties, is really the story of one man: Francis Marion "Borax" Smith. Like his Civil War "Swamp Fox" namesake, Smith was everywhere. After making millions mining borax in Death Valley, he teamed up with F.C. Havens, who had no dearth of ideas to spend Smith's money. First they bought up all the independent rail lines they could find. Then they started a system of electric street railroads in 1893.

Well before the Bay Area Rapid Transit (BART) thought of it, Smith wanted to tunnel under the bay to reach San Francisco and compete with the Southern Pacific railroad. When the Army Corps of Engineers rejected the idea, he developed a new, improved ferry fleet, built a 3.5-mile trestle out to deep water in order to reduce travel time to the city, extended the streetcar rails to meet the ferry, coupled as many as eight cars to handle the volume of people, and painted everything bright orange. He promised a 35-minute ride to San Francisco when the first trains left University and Shattuck avenues in Berkeley on October 26, 1903.

"Borax" called the whole system the Key Route because (1) the long trestle and ferry slips looked like a key and (2) he considered it the key to Bay Area transit problems. In the next few years, he expanded the system to Dwight Way and then Ashby Avenue up to the Claremont Hotel.

But by 1913, Smith had overextended himself and filed for bankruptcy. His trains and ferries still thrived though under the direction of others—thrived until the advent of the internal combustion engine. Buses started to replace streetcars by 1921, and ferries began transporting automobiles across the bay in 1929. When the Bay Bridge was built in 1937, the death knell for the Key Route was sounding. The last Key System train left Berkeley station, carrying a gaggle of local dignitaries, in 1958.

It took a big earthquake in October, 1989, to disable the Bay Bridge, and temporarily bring trans-bay passenger ferry service back to the East Bay. Somewhere, "Borax" Smith must have been saying "I told you so."

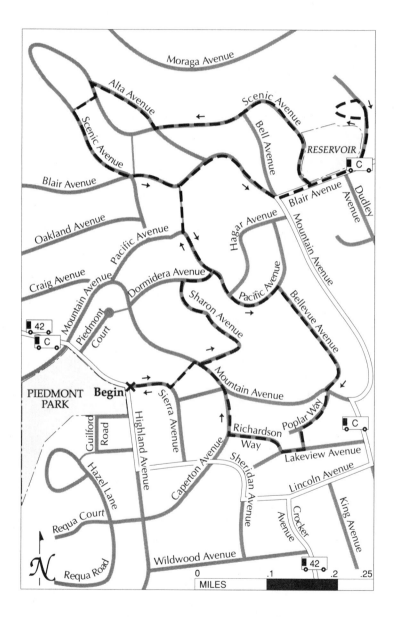

17

Piedmont Hi-Lines

Terrain: *moderate to steep; improved paths and steps*
Bus line: *Piedmont "C" from MacArthur BART station*
Parks: *Piedmont Park, Lake Merritt near Grand Avenue*
Shops: *Grand and Lakeshore Avenues in Oakland*
Distance: *3.3 miles*
Directions: *From 580, take Oakland Avenue exit and follow past Grand Avenue to Highland Avenue in Piedmont. Turn right to center of town and Piedmont Park a few blocks away.*

None of the footpaths in Piedmont are marked, or named, which probably says something about the town's receptivity to foreign walkers—foreign being anyone who lives outside of Piedmont. Do not fear though. The paths covered in this walk are public pathways and the only laws governing their use are moral ones, dictating respect for private property and personal privacy. So feel free not only to walk these paths but to look, smell, touch, and think as well.

Piedmont, too, is a town that doesn't wait for its government to improve itself. Several residents cut through red tape and chipped in some $40,000 to build the mission-style bus stop on Highland Avenue at the center of town. This may be the classiest bus stop in the Bay Area.

This walk begins on Sierra Avenue just off Highland across from Piedmont Park's Community Hall. Take the path next to

#17 Sierra (look for an iron post with no sign). This ivy corridor brings you to Mt. Sharon Street (notice the handsome brick house two doors down on the left that looks like it could have been transported whole from Revolutionary War Valley Forge) where you bear left. A right on Dormidera Street and a left on Pacific Avenue leads you to steep steps with a center rail and a beautiful redwood house, built in the First Bay Tradition, to the right. Ascend past a large gray house on the hillside, built in no particular tradition, with a tenuous arrangement of concrete blocks and wooden posts for its foundation.

Walk right on Blair Avenue up to the East Bay Municipal Utility District (EBMUD) reservoir just past Scenic Avenue. It's a covered reservoir so you won't see any water. Continue past, first, a small rest area then another of Piedmont's nicely designed and functional bus stops. The path leaves the sidewalk, skirting the EBMUD facility, passing through a small redwood grove. Proceed up to the locked gate on your left, go right, then right again back onto the path leading out to Blair. It may feel like more due to the climb, but you've only covered about one mile so far.

Now it's mostly all downhill as you go right on Scenic with the reservoir and fenced EBMUD forest on the right. Bear right on Alta Avenue, a narrow street with no sidewalks, to expansive views of San Francisco, Mt. Tamalpais in Marin, and the North Bay. The white-lattice, ivy-covered fence at #130 adds to the scenery.

Alta rejoins Scenic at a circle where a left leads to steps just beyond #304 that head down to the winding Scenic Avenue. Hold onto the iron rail on either side in case you become distracted by the great views of city skylines, Lake Merritt, the Bay Bridge, the Marin hills, the South Bay, as well as an array of redwood fences and shingled roofs along the way. Notice, too, the house at #150 Scenic, built in the First Bay Tradition.

At the intersection, go left on Blair, but before doing so walk about 100 feet to the right to see 575 Blair, one house from the corner. Although modified, renovated, and looking nothing like the original, this house was Piedmont's first, built by Rev. Joseph Worcester, rented by Jack London, painted by William Keith, and peeked into by Bernard Maybeck, inspiring that architect to develop his brown-shingled, rustic style.

Continue up the south side of Blair to the steps next to #622—the same ones you came up previously—and descend to Pacific. Stay on Pacific and as it bends to the left, turn right on mansion-lined Bellevue Avenue. This is the heart of grand Piedmont, with good examples of the kind of affluence and style Piedmont is known for. At #50, an elegant classic; at #37, expansive grounds, with a lively fountain; at #20, unusual 20-light leaded-glass windows.

At the bottom of the street, there's a perfect redwood in the center of the intersection. Bear left around the tree to tiny Poplar Way. Keep bearing left on Poplar, past palms and redwoods, then go right at Lakeview Avenue and right at Richardson Way, passing two Tudor Revival houses. Turn right on Caperton Avenue, which flows into Mountain Avenue. Admire the diamond-pane windows of another era at #280, then take the path with the rose-colored concrete path just past #270 on the left. This path is directly across from #255, a sprawling stucco giant with a delicate flowered urn in the center of the entrance stairway.

The path leads to Sierra, where a right takes you back to Piedmont Park across Highland. At the crosswalk at Sierra and Highland enter the park and see the commemorative plaque of the Piedmont Beautification Foundation embedded in a boulder. It's a foundation that has obviously kept very busy over the years.

"The Simple Home"

A movement toward a simpler, a truer, a more vital art expression, is now taking place in California. It is a movement which involves painters and poets, composers and sculptors, and only lacks co-ordination to give it a significant influence upon modern life. One of the first steps in this movement, it seems to me, should be to introduce more widely the thought of the simple home — to emphasize the gospel of the simple life, to scatter broadcast the faith in simple beauty, to make prevalent the conviction that we must *live* art before we can create it. . . .

Having determined the general form of construction in wood, it is next important to consider its right treatment and handling. Wood is a good material if left in the natural finish, but it is generally spoiled by the use of paint or varnish. This is a matter which perhaps cannot be entirely reasoned out. It must be seen and felt to be understood; and yet it is a point vital to artistic work. There is a refinement and character about natural wood which is entirely lost when the surface is altered by varnish and polish. Oil paint is the most deadly foe of an artistic wood treatment. It is hard and characterless, becoming dull and grimy with time and imparting a cold severity to the walls. . . .

As to the second reason for treating wood with paint, ornamentation, let us consider for a moment wherein lies the beauty of a house. We are too prone to forget that a single house is but a detail in a landscape. In either case its effect should never be considered apart from the whole. The exterior of a house should always be conceived so that it will harmonize with its surroundings. The safest means of effecting this is by leaving the natural material to the tender care of the elements. Wood in time weathers to a soft brown or gray in which the shadows are the chief marks of accent. The tones are sufficiently neutral to accord with any landscape, and the only criticism from an artistic point of view which can be made upon the coloring of such a group of houses is that they are rather sober and reserved. California has a remedy for this defect in the abundance of climbing flowers. Banksia rose, ivy-geranium, Wistaria [sic], clematis, passion vine, Ampelopsis, and a joyous host of companion vines are ready to enliven any sober wall. Wire-mesh screens a foot from the house will protect the shingles from dampness, and our houses can thus be decked as for a carnival in a wealth of varying bloom.

Charles Keeler, from *The Simple Home,* 1904

Kensington

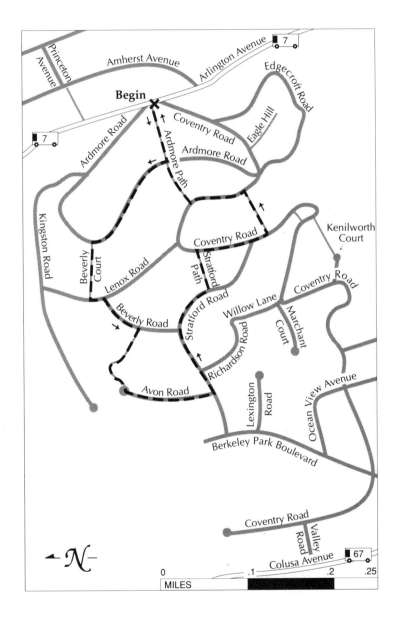

Princeton Avenue

Amherst Avenue

Arlington Avenue

7

Edgecroft Road

Begin

Coventry Road

Eagle Hill

Ardmore Road

7

Ardmore Path

Ardmore Road

Kingston Road

Coventry Road

Kenilworth Court

Beverly Court

Lenox Road

Coventry Road

Stratford Path

Coventry Road

Beverly Road

Stratford Road

Willow Lane

Marchant Court

Richardson Road

Avon Road

Lexington Road

Ocean View Avenue

Berkeley Park Boulevard

N

Coventry Road

Valley Road

Colusa Avenue

67

0   .1   .2   .25

MILES

18

Below the Hayward Fault

Terrain: *easy; improved lanes and steps; unimproved lanes*
Bus line: *7*
Parks: *Tilden and Wildcat Regional Parks, Blake Gardens, John Hinkel Park, Kensington Youth Hut and Park (just past the shopping district on Arlington)*
Shopping: *Arlington Avenue, Colusa Circle shopping area, nearby Berkeley areas on Solano and Walnut Square*
Distance: *1 mile*
Directions: *From the Marin Avenue circle, take Arlington Avenue to the center of town.*

Touching borders with four other East Bay towns, Kensington is one of the area's few unincorporated communities. It depends on Contra Costa County, with its government based in distant Martinez, to fill its potholes and repair the cracks widened by the whims of the Hayward Fault. According to one longtime resident, though, "Most of our streets are so dangerous, we have to be careful in using them. The old-timer becomes inured to the sharp uphill, downhill turns, the swinging in and around the cars. But for the newcomer it is a harrowing first-time experience. However, in time he or she, with great nonchalance, will also whip the curves and dodge the cars. Our on-street parking problems defy description."

It is also a town of captivating lanes, winding, quiet streets, and older, established homes — many of the First Bay Tradition developed by turn-of-the-century architects like Bernard Maybeck and Julia Morgan — with views of the bay or the surrounding hills. This walk takes in many of these features, and is probably safer than driving those aforementioned streets.

Start across from the main shopping area on Arlington Avenue. Just behind a small public parking lot take the Ardmore Path down the steps, noticeably cracked from earthquake movements, then widening into an elegant lane with a landscaped median strip and bordered by a sprawling pine. It is one of the East Bay's grandest hidden pedestrian promenades.

Exit onto Ardmore Avenue and turn right, noticing the rustic and First Bay Tradition bungalows at #114 and #124. Go left at Beverly Court, which is easy to miss but is marked by an attractive craftsman wooden sign and post next to #97. This small street seems very private but is, in fact, public. It narrows into a walking lane straight ahead connecting with Lenox Road. Go left, then very soon take a right onto Beverly Road. Just past #40 take a right onto an unmarked paved drive that again looks private but is a public way that faces the hillside above. This leads into Avon Road, which ends at Stratford Road.

Go left on Stratford and follow until it bends to the right where you must look closely for the wooden post and sign marking the Stratford Path. Take this hidden, tranquil footpath to Coventry Road and a lacy pepper tree. Walk to the right and just before #636, ascend the steps to the left, looking back at bay views, wild gardens, and simple houses. At the top, where it joins the curving Coventry Road again, there's a small wooden bench for a breather.

A left on Coventry takes you back to a part of the Ardmore Path not covered before. It is unmarked so look for it next to #719. Ascend to Ardmore Road then promenade on the magnanimous upper Ardmore Path to the start.

Kensington: The Volunteer Town

S ince it was developed in 1911, Kensington has remained unincorporated, a tiny 1.6-square-mile principality of 5,000, tucked in a corner of its sovereign, and sometimes absentee, landlord, Contra Costa County. Locals may scoff, but county supervisors refer to the community technically as a service district.

Being unincorporated means it doesn't have its own legally recognized government, yet Kensington may be, in practice, more incorporated than most incorporated towns. And the reason for that is volunteers, which the little town is bursting with.

First, there's the Kensington Community Council, an umbrella agency which coordinates such things as recreational programs for youth and adults, the Friends of the Library, the Scouts, *Outlook*, a community newspaper that's been running for almost fifty years, after-school enrichment programs, and special programs like "A History of Afro-American Song," complemented by special performers. And they do it all with private donations and regular fund-raisers.

Then there's the Kensington Improvement Club, which works like a local planning agency. The members sponsor landscaping projects, design traffic median strips, and lobby the county government in Martinez for particular ordinances and building variances.

Then, too, there's the Kensington Property Owners Association, which does similar things as the Improvement Club, along with sponsoring a crime-watch program in conjunction with the police.

Oh yes, there's the police. The chief runs the meetings of the Community Service District, a board of three elected, and unpaid, Kensington citizens who are in turn accountable to the county. The county, through property taxes, pays the full-time police and fire departments, but when Proposition 13 was passed, cutting budgets drastically, townsfolk went ahead and voted in a special tax to be added to their property taxes to make up for the deficiencies. Kensington is the only town in California to have added this special assessment. It's not a requirement of the assessment, but when you call the police station, the chief, himself, usually answers.

The Kensington Municipal Advisory Council rounds out this remarkable volunteer government. This group advises the county planning department on local zoning and variance issues.

Everyone, including interested citizens, meets once a year in November at the annual town hall meeting, which the Improvement Club hosted in 1989. It was shifted to the school auditorium in anticipation of a large turnout. Seems the financially strapped, adjacent Richmond School District wanted to sell a big piece of open space it owns to developers. The land is in Kensington and abuts Kensington Park, the community's primary recreation spot. The community wants a major say in what will be done with the land, the preference being to leave it in open space. You can be sure Kensington will speak out loud and "volun-clear."

Albany

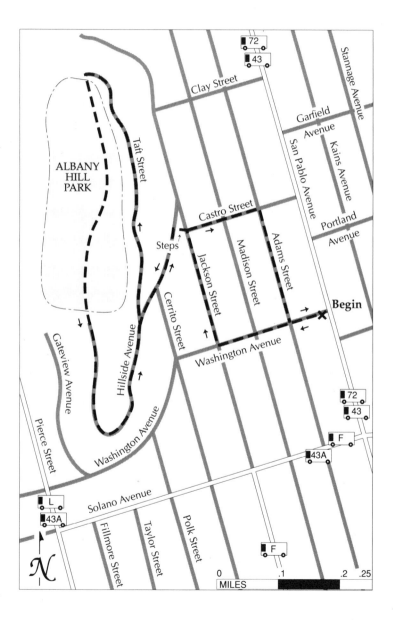

19

The Presidents' Hike to the Top

Terrain: *easy to moderate; improved steps, unimproved trails*
Bus line: *72M*
Parks: *Albany Hill Park, Vista School Playground, Creekside Park on north side of Albany Hill*
Shops: *lower Solano Avenue, San Pablo Avenue north and south of Solano, El Cerrito Shopping Center south on San Pablo*
Distance: *1.8 miles*
Directions: *From I-80, either direction, take Albany exit to San Pablo Avenue, turn left to Washington Street.*

According to the fact sheet provided by its chamber of commerce, Albany covers 5 square miles—1.7 square miles of land and 3.3 square miles of water. Of the part of the town that is land, only 10 percent is vacant, and you'll see and amble through most of it on this walk.

Despite its proximity to the more cosmopolitan cities of the Bay Area, Albany, in some ways, feels like the town that time forgot: the Lake Wobegon of the East Bay. There are 2.18 persons per household, approximately 13 persons per acre, not a mansion in sight, and the hottest news this week, for example, reported in the police blotter of the local weekly, is an anonymous complaint of long-haired hippies doing suspicious things in a car. On this occasion, the police investigated the call and found three rather gentle students playing chess in their van. It's a family kind of town and this is a family kind of walk.

Start on Washington Street (where else would you start on a Presidents' walk?) just off San Pablo Avenue. Head west past Adams Street, then Madison Street, (both were in favor of westward expansion, I believe) then go right on Jackson Street (Old Hickory would've taken any direction no one else was going). Just beyond the Vista School see the concrete steps on the left opposite Castro Street (other Western Hemisphere presidents are included, although Albany, I'm sure, didn't name this street after Fidel). Climb these steps and turn left onto Hillside Avenue. Here are views of the East Bay, looking back for a change, taking in El Cerrito, Albany, Berkeley, and the Bay Area Rapid Transit (BART).

Go straight, past Cerrito Street (named after the great, yet clandestine, President L. Cerrito — actually *cerrito* means "little hill"), then turn right on Taft Street (Republican Taft would have liked a turn to the right but may have had difficulty ascending his namesake street, given his ample girth). Albany Hill Park rises steeply to the left, and you could attempt a shortcut there, up a rough trail, if you're a good scrambler, are in shape, and are in a hurry.

Otherwise, continue on Taft, viewing the corporations and monopolies below on San Pablo, and Grizzly Peak in the hills above Berkeley (which was named for one of the last grizzly bears in the Bay Area, shot near a spring on the peak where it lived). At the top of Taft, there's an automobile turnaround and the entrance to six-acre Albany Hill Park, marked with a sign to the left. The park owes it existence to citizens who fought against developers and public utilities proposing all kinds of schemes over the years to either build on the hill or level it for fill. The last battle involved the building of high-rise apartments on the west side, mitigated by the setting aside of four-acre

Creekside Park, with its native oak forest, an open stretch of Cerrito Creek, and a rough trail leading to the top of Albany Hill Park.

Enter the dirt trail past the gate, rising gently with the drone of freeway traffic below and the quiet bay beyond. With mostly eucalyptus trees all around (the town's official history states they were planted "to lessen the danger from explosions of a dynamite plant," which may leave you, as me, scratching your head and marveling at how politicians have always tried to butter every burnt side they could), continue straight to the top, 338 feet above sea level, stopping to rest, perhaps, at the bench to the left overlooking the hills or the two benches on the bay side.

A little farther is a very substantial iron cross, with built-in fluorescent lights, erected by the Albany Lions (what Garrison Keillor could do with that one!). Religious holiday services are still occasionally held at the cross, which does not violate the separation of church and state since it sits on a thin slice of private property.

Beyond the cross, the trail bends to the right, veering away from the houses ahead, as it drops toward the bay. At a clearing about a hundred feet down, take the first small dirt footpath to the left, which leads to Hillside Avenue. Golden Gate Fields racetrack comes into view as the street bears to the left, continuing past fairly modern houses, designed with one thing in mind: the view. Stay on Hillside, past Cerrito, with the Vista School and its playground below. Its jungle gym, slide, and tire swings could be a good diversion if you have young children along.

Just past the cyclone fence, take the steps down to Jackson and continue on Castro, noting the whimsical pig weather vane at #956. Go right on Adams (which side of the aisle was *he* on?), admiring the distinctive craftsman bungalows at #725 and #729, before returning to Washington — where all political speeches and Presidents' walks should return.

Cedric Wright on Trees

Consider the life of trees.

Aside from the axe, what trees acquire from man is
inconsiderable.

What man may acquire from trees is immeasurable.

From their mute forms there flows a poise, in silence, a
lovely sound and motion in response to wind.

What peace comes to those aware of the voice and
bearing of trees!

Trees do not scream for attention.

A tree, a rock, has no pretence, only a real growth out
of itself, in close communion with the universal spirit.

A tree retains a deep serenity.

It establishes in the earth not only its root system but
also those roots of its beauty and its unknown
consciousness.

Sometimes one may sense a glisten of that consciousness,
and with such perspective, feel that man is not
necessarily the highest form of life.

Tree qualities, after long communion, come to reside in man.

As stillness enhances sound, so through little things
the joy of living expands.

One is aware, lying under trees,

of the roots and directions of one's whole being.

Perceptions drift in from earth and sky.

A vast healing begins.

From *Words of the Earth,* 1960
(with permission from Sierra Club Books)

Cedric Wright, born in 1889, was an early Sierra Club enthu-
siast, noted mountain photographer, and a teacher of the violin
at Mills College. He lived in Berkeley, in a house designed by
Bernard Maybeck, during a period of cultural and environmental

renaissance in the Bay Area. In a foreword to *Words of the Earth,* which the Sierra Club published as a memorial to Wright, the great landscape photographer Ansel Adams wrote, "Cedric believed that any man's spiritual horizon would be expanded through contact with nature, and his life was dedicated to this idea. . . . He had little use for the self-protective conventional wisdoms [sic]. He paid a price to live with his convictions, but it kept his genius intact and lost him none of the affection of his friends."

Mill Valley around the turn of the century. (PHOTO COURTESY OF MILL VALLEY
PUBLIC LIBRARY.)

Mill Valley

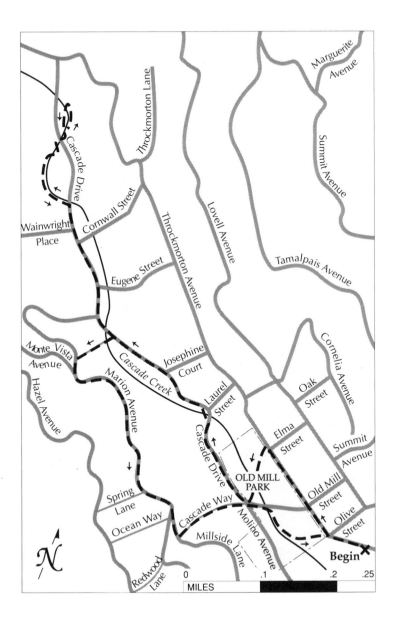

MILES

20

Cascade Creek, Valley, & Falls

Terrain: *easy to steep; improved steps and bridges; unimproved trails*
Special equipment: *shoes with good traction*
Bus line: *10*
Parks: *Old Mill Park*
Shops: *downtown Mill Valley*
Distance: *3 miles*
Directions: *From Route 101 going north from Golden Gate Bridge, take Mill Valley exit, stay straight past the Route 1 turn, follow Miller Avenue into the center of town. From Route 101 going south from Richmond-San Rafael Bridge, take East Blithedale Avenue exit and follow that street straight into Mill Valley.*

C ascade Creek played a big part in Mill Valley's origins, as it provided water power for John Reed's sawmill, a replica of which you will see on this walk in Old Mill Park. The creek is a quieter one now since water from it has been dammed and diverted for a managed water supply, but the waterfall, farther upstream, called Cascade Falls, may be the loveliest in the Bay Area. About 3,000 years ago ancestors of local Coast Miwok Indians settled in this valley after a 30-year migration from Siberia. This walk will show why they and the Spaniards, Europeans, and Americans after them stayed.

Start on Throckmorton Avenue just past the center of town. Samuel Throckmorton had owned much of Mill Valley in the last century but, in 1883, died in debt and foreclosure of most of his land. The bank repossessed 13,000 acres, which soon became the heart of Mill Valley.

Walk past Olive Street, then Old Mill Street, past the art deco facade of the Old Mill School. The school site and Old Mill Park across the street were part of the original plan for the town designed in the late 1870s by Michael M. O'Shaughnessy, the engineer who built Hetch Hetchy Dam and designed many San Francisco streets. A designed town was a new concept in those days.

Continue up past the Mill Valley Public Library, an architecturally acclaimed building, on the left side of the street. It's one of the most inviting libraries in the Bay Area, a place where you can read, sitting on a redwood deck overlooking a lush forested park. Go left into the building's small parking lot to stairs leading down into the redwood park that adjoins it. Follow a fairly nondescript trail down to the creek and, if the water is low, cross it on stepping stones. If you'd like a tamer way of crossing, continue on the trail straight to Old Mill Street and turn right, taking the wooden footbridge, across the street, spanning Cascade Creek.

Either way, then bear right onto Cascade Drive, which follows the course of Cascade Creek. Just past the California bungalow at #83, cross the creek via another path and wooden footbridge, continuing on Cascade to the left.

The street climbs the foothills on the southeastern side of Mt. Tamalpais, through groves of redwoods and houses that seem very comfortable with each other. The creek meanders and alternates between the left and right side of the road.

Pass Marion Avenue, then Eugene Street with its old concrete bridge and young redwoods, clustered like a fairy ring. Shortly after Wainright Place, the road narrows and the houses become more Hobbit-like. A small creekside park appears on the left, allowing a chance to whisper closer greetings to the creek.

The Lundquist family at Three Wells, Cascade Creek and Canyon, Mill Valley circa 1890. (PHOTO COURTESY MILL VALLEY LIBRARY.)

A short distance from here, just after an old concrete bridge and opposite #30, see the sign "Three Wells" on a tree and take the dirt trail down to the left beside the creek. Continue along the cool banks of the creek around a sandbagged corner to where the sound of the water intensifies. Go up and around the bend and you're at the three wells—deep depressions in the creek bed, creating a three-level waterfall that during the rainy season is spectacular. The water runs year-round, so it's a good place to soak your feet on a hot day or meditate by the water or have a snack or for just about anything quiet.

Farther up the trail is a wood bridge that crosses the creek, continuing under a wooden overpass/walkway for the redwood-slat house above. Cross another wooden bridge and then climb up onto and across Cascade Drive to the trail straight ahead marked "Cascade Falls." Stay right where the redwood- and laurel-lined trail forks, cross a sturdy bridge, and go up a slight incline to see the pristine falls. There's a bench, as well as other vantage points, to contemplate the falling ribbon of water and the pool that it feeds.

When ready, climb the trail to the right to a point above the falls, cross the creek on a wooden footbridge going left, and soon connect with a wider trail on the other side of the creek. Retrace your steps to the Three Wells trail, starting to the left of the phone pole, and return on this wild stretch of Cascade Creek back out to Cascade Road. Proceed to the right, noticing the care taken in building around redwood trees at #310, as well as other forest houses Bernard Maybeck would have loved.

Pass Cornwall Street and Eugene, then shortly beyond Marion look for a path at the end of an old wooden fence just after #183 and before #175 (with its shingled entrance gate marked "Breidablik"). A telephone pole on Cascade also marks the entrance to this path. Turn right on this right of way, over an old worn bridge, then up a rough root and rock trail, skirting closely past the house on the left to a more organized section of stone and wood-plank steps leading out and onto Marion Avenue. (If you should miss this trail or don't have the proper footgear, walking up Marion will take you to the same spot.)

Turn left on Marion, continuing to walk up, bearing left past Monte Vista Avenue, keeping in mind you're on the way to a very pleasing descent in a short while. The road winds past an assortment of hillside homes and valley views until it reaches a fork with Millside Lane to the left and signs pointing to Mt. Tamalpais destinations to the right. Stay on the winding Millside to Cascade Way, marked on the left just past the cedar-shingled roof of #7. Here you go down, thankfully, 310 steps of varying materials, built over a water runoff that eventually drains into Cascade Creek. The Cascade Way is part of the Dipsea Trail and the annual 7.1-mile Dipsea Race from Mill Valley to Stinson

Beach. Back at the previously mentioned fork some 400 more steps of the Trail continue up and connect with trails that lead to the top of Mt. Tamalpais. It's a grueling foot race that draws some 1,500 participants a year. It was started in 1903 by members of the San Francisco Olympic Club.

At the bottom, Cascade Way becomes a small street that soon intersects with Cascade Drive and Molino Avenue. Cross at the yellow striped crosswalk to the wooden bridge over the creek and into Old Mill Park. Stay right along the creek to view the open-sided, shingled-roof structure that marks the spot where John Reed built his sawmill in 1834. This looks like it could be the original but it's actually an old replica. A nineteenth-century sawmill needed torrents of water to operate, which proves Cascade Creek had a much higher water level at that time.

Continue through the redwood park or enjoy the playground equipment or refresh yourself in the shingled, redwood rest rooms, finally exiting onto Throckmorton and Olive streets. Sam Throckmorton would probably have drawn some consolation to see how his repossessed 13,000 acres were eventually developed.

The Birth & Growth of Mill Valley

M ill Valley owes its founding to two factors: redwoods and the railroad. Its first settler, John Thomas Reed, built a sawmill in 1836 along Cascade Creek in one of three canyons of giant redwoods at the southeastern base of Mount Tamalpais. The demand for his supply of redwood lumber came from the Presidio in San Francisco, and his Mexican land grant was called Rancho Corte Madera del Presidio or "where the wood is cut for the Presidio."

By 1889, there were still more cattle than people, but that year, to service a popular resort, the railroad built a spur of the Pacific Northern. The endeavor was choreographed by developer and financier Joseph Eastland as part of his newly formed Tamalpais Land and Water Company. He soon commissioned plans for a one-square-mile community, and a year later lots went up for public auction. Eastland even named the town after himself, but residents insisted on Mill Valley after a period of contention when both names were used simultaneously.

Not only did Eastland lose out on naming the town after himself, but no streets have been named for him either. One Outdoor Art Club founding member attributes this to the town's longtime anti-growth sentiments, while Eastland represented the other side of the coin. "We fought every improvement," she said in the Mill Valley Historical Society News, "even street lights to keep Mill Valley the way it was." In contrast, and perhaps defiance, Eastland was the first in town to have electricity installed in his home.

In 1896, the Mount Tamalpais Scenic Railroad, "the crookedest railroad in the world," opened for business (it lasted until 1931), thrilling tourists to a winding ride up the mountain, and prompting the building of more resorts, boarding houses, stores, and saloons to service them. By 1900, the town voted to incorporate, mostly to stop the spread of more saloons. And two years later, to stop the destruction of redwoods and native plants, women of the town formed the Outdoor Art Club.

A good thing, because after the 1906 San Francisco earthquake, Mill Valley began to grow at a faster pace. The opening of the Golden Gate Bridge in 1937 brought further growth and many permanent residents. The sixties spawned flower children, communes, and natural foods stores. And the real estate boom of the eighties made the town more upscale.

But Mill Valley is still a haven for writers and other independent-minded people. There are no noticeable saloons in town, and though most of the cattle have retreated to West Marin, the turn-of-the-century atmosphere of original buildings, natural places, and (mostly) easy going people, make the "Switzerland of America" a very agreeable place.

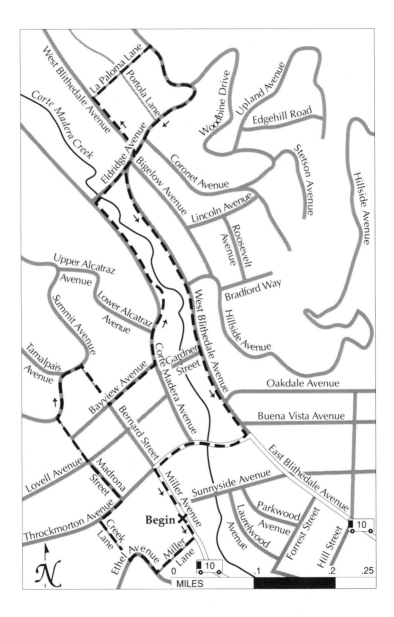

21

Mill Valley Lanes

Terrain: *easy to moderate; improved paths, steps, sidewalks and streets, unimproved paths and trails*
Bus line: *10 (Golden Gate Transit)*
Parks: *Old Mill Park, The Depot in the center of town*
Shops: *Miller and Throckmorton Avenues in center of Mill Valley*
Distance: *1.7 miles*
Directions: *From Route 101 going north from Golden Gate Bridge, take Mill Valley exit. Stay straight past the Route 1 turn, follow Miller Avenue into the center of town. From Route 101 going south from Richmond-San Rafael Bridge, take East Blithedale Avenue exit and follow that street straight into Mill Valley.*

Set in a valley at the foot of Mt. Tamalpais, Mill Valley in Marin County has been called the "Switzerland of America." Like Berkeley and its ever-vigilant Hillside Club, Mill Valley had its own Outdoor Art Club, organized at the turn of the century by some of the townswomen, initially to stem the destruction of redwoods, native plants, and flowers. They did that and also influenced the style of buildings in the center of town, many of which are still standing. Bernard Maybeck designed their clubhouse, at the edge of the town square, in 1905 (which you'll see at the end of this walk).

The layout of the town as you see it today was no accident. When a branch of the railroad came in 1889, a realty company laid out a one-square-mile community including parks, stairways, a town square, a school, and three church sites. This walk covers much of that original town site, and the lanes and stairways offer good views of this town that looks like a mountain village in the Alps.

The walk starts on Miller Avenue near the center of town at Mill Creek Plaza, a commercial development next to #38 Miller. At the end of the parking lot, find solid wooden steps, known as Miller Lane but without a sign, and climb up through a redwood and eucalyptus hillside grove. The steps change to concrete and wood planks, and with a wood railing, the ascent is fairly steep but easy. Wood stairs at the end lift you onto Ethel Avenue, a narrow trail that might have been better labeled a lane. Turn right, enjoying choice views of Mt. Tamalpais and the foothills, before coming to a set of concrete steps, with two iron rails, on the right. This is Creek Lane, and, like most of the paths in town, has no sign. The stump beside it is marked with #95.

Soon wood steps replace the concrete as you drop to a parking lot and a continuation of Creek Lane out to Throckmorton Avenue. Turn right, then left at the next street, Madrona Avenue. One block up is Lovell Avenue, where, opposite Madrona, you'll find an unmarked pathway — a set of broken concrete steps next to #52 — leading up past a small side street, Bayview Avenue, to improved wood and concrete steps rising onto Summit Avenue.

Bear right, taking extra care to walk close to the right side of this street which has no sidewalk. There are picturesque views of the village below and bay beyond, but instead of walking and looking at the same time, it may be best to stop, move safely off the street, and admire the sight. Fortunately, it's only a short distance around the bend to the wooden stairs (no sign) on the right, where Tamalpais Avenue connects with Summit. It's at the crosswalk, just before #110. The path slices through woodsy gardens and backyards, finishing with wooden steps down to

Bayview Avenue. If you walk softly along the way, a very friendly cat may prance up to greet you with the cat equivalent to a Marin hug.

Go left on curving Bayview to the four corners at the bottom, then straight on Corte Madera Avenue past Lower Alcatraz Place. At this point, Corte Madera narrows considerably with only one-way auto traffic permitted out. Walking this short stretch is possible, but a better way, commonly used by pedestrians, is a pathway to the right and below the street. It's a right-of-way and driveway that enters a cool, natural area of redwoods, laurels, and the Corte Madera Creek. On a hot day this would be a wonderful picnic spot.

Shortly, the path returns to Corte Madera Avenue, which is equally cool and almost as natural. Environmentally harmonious houses line the street, and one, #160, built in 1891 and named Redwood Lodge, is particularly handsome, with redwood groves and a stone wall border that was built with obvious care and skill. At Eldridge Avenue, turn right and cross the bridge, noting the attractive gingerbread houses on this short but intriguing street. Bear left around the corner onto West Blithedale Avenue. (Careful here! Cars coming toward you have a stop sign, but there is no sidewalk so stay close to the curb.)

Continue on the sidewalk on the north side of busy West Blithedale up Blithedale Canyon, a historical section of town that was once the site of the popular Blithedale Hotel and the Mt. Tamalpais Scenic Railroad, which snaked to the top of Mt. Tam in the early part of the twentieth century. Within a half block, take the crosswalk leading to La Paloma Lane, marked with a sign on the other side of the street. The asphalt lane runs between two wooden fences, crosses tiny Portola Lane, and then continues as a dirt and broken-asphalt trail to steps leading up to Eldridge Avenue. Turn right, noting the attractive stone work and wall at #108, walking past Woodbine Drive as the street bends to the right, joining West Blithedale and Bigelow.

This is a fairly busy intersection and is not walker-friendly, so approach it with caution. Bear left onto West Blithedale, and either follow the tamer sidewalk, cut through a grove of redwoods, on the south side, or cross and enter the wilder dirt path into the small natural area next to Corte Madera Creek. This short path leads back out to West Blithedale.

The redwoods, creek, and some older houses make the auto traffic almost tolerable on this short stretch of West Blithedale. And, where it meets Throckmorton, you can admire the striking Our Lady of Mount Carmel church across the street, and the Outdoor Art Club's Bernard Maybeck–designed clubhouse at #1 West Blithedale on the corner. The clubhouse's rustic, weathered fence, colorful garden, old native trees, and whimsical whale faces carved into the trellis columns over the patio entrance reflect the famous architect's spirit — a spirit which sets the tone for this Alpine-like Marin town that is growing old gracefully.

A right on Throckmorton, past the art deco movie theater across the street, brings you back over the creek and into the past and present hub of Mill Valley, where this walk started.

Spring

*T*he notion of spring in February is a difficult one for a former New Englander. Old friends just shake their heads lamenting the loss of their comrade in cold. Yet gradually, East Coast roots fade into February cherry blossoms and pussy willows, which seem to be more inherently compatible to humans than ice, snow, slush, and cold.

Spring in the Bay Area is a gentle affair. Not so much a burst of bud and blossom but a progression. It doesn't arise from death and dormancy; rather, a well-groomed bon vivant, it puts on dressier clothes and steps out more. Cherry and plum blossoms are the first arrivals. Delicate and sweet-smelling, they embroider neighborhood streets. They add variety and luster to the many hues of green painted by winter rains. They brighten a cloudy day; and when their brilliance wanes, their falling petals lighten the dark, wet paths.

The cherry blossoms smell sweet, and the spring air is cool, fresh, and alive. For a moment, no thought intrudes. The boundaries disappear. There is "no-thing" in the way. There is peace.

In the gardens, purple crocuses appear — quite suddenly — and in the hills, small shoots of green rise among deadened stalks and branches. The feeling is one of rising, a welling up, an expansiveness to fill up the dead spaces left by winter. If the universe is ever-expanding, as some say, this is an expression of it.

Each year spring appears as if this were the first time, the first spring. Nature seems surprised — delighted in a way — without memory of how it was or how it should be. And without this retention of past images, there is unbridled budding and flowering.

Deep inside, there is flowering, too — deep beneath the layers of memory and programmed thought. Deep beneath ideas of life, there is life itself, unburdened by meanings or messages, dogma or belief, hope or despair. It is just there — a bud opening ever so gently in spring — gently yet fearlessly, without doubt or hesitation.

To walk in nature as it blooms in spring nurtures the spirit. The camellia — so full with flowers that it drips petals. A new iris braving the early spring cold and rain. Daffodils dressed to the hilt like little girls parading about in their mother's party dress and high heels. And wildflowers reveling like Mardi Gras mummers on the hillsides and shorelines.

It takes a certain slowness to see. Scurrying about, thinking of this and that, obscures the view. For only as the mind quiets can its view, both inner and outer, deepen. And only as that view deepens, can the spring inside match the spring outside.

Sausalito

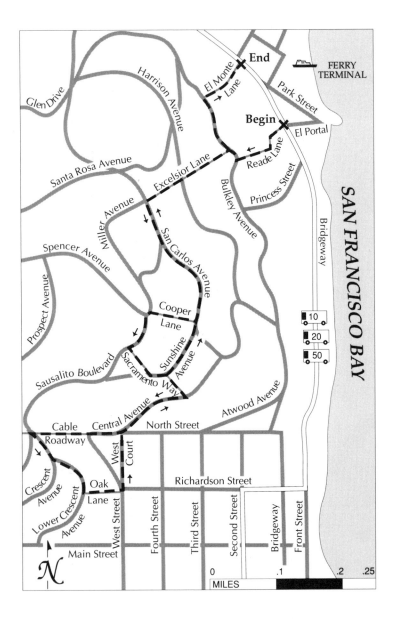

22

High-Stepping Loop

Terrain: *moderate to steep; improved lanes and steps, unimproved steps and paths*
Bus line: *10 (Golden Gate Transit)*
Parks: *Sausalito Civic Center, several small parks and rest areas along the waterfront off Bridgeway Boulevard and Front Street*
Shops: *Along Bridgeway Boulevard*
Distance: *1.9 miles*
Directions: *From 101, take Sausalito exit to Bridgeway and center of town.*

Sausalito, today, is associated with style, affluence, and "the good life." But at the turn of the century, the town evoked images of rowdy saloons, cutthroat characters, and bordellos. The hills above the downtown section, though, have always been quieter, more genteel — a haven removed from the busy world below, and beyond, across the Golden Gate. This walk starts where all the action is then takes you up to a Sausalito of peaceful lanes, gardens, watchful cats, old Victorians, and pleasing views.

Start at Reade Lane, marked with a sign at Bridgeway Boulevard opposite El Portal Street in the heart of the downtown district. It's directly across from the small park and decorative fountain called Plaza Vina Del Mar. In 1898, it would have been risky walking this alleyway, but today it's much safer as its steps rise and zigzag to views of Richardson and San Francisco Bays. It opens to a wider lane near the top, exiting onto Bulkley Avenue next to a plaque commemorating "The Founders' Tree," a cypress, saved from destruction by ten turn-of-the-century women who joined hands around the tree. The act led to the forming of the Sausalito Women's Club, and, according to the plaque, evolved into one of the first programs "to legally recognize and preserve the beauties of nature." The original tree is gone, but the club still thrives.

Next to the site is the First Presbyterian Church, and directly across from the church are stone steps and an iron railing. Take this path, which is called Excelsior Lane, crossing Harrison Avenue, continuing straight up the steps and lane to San Carlos Avenue. Go left—taking care while walking on this fairly busy street without sidewalks—past the brown-shingled #121 with its ivy-covered fence, past Spencer Avenue, past the multistoried, brown-shingled house at #93, until you reach Cooper Lane, marked with a sign, just beyond #63 on the right.

Climb the concrete steps to a stone and gravel path that leads to the juncture of Sausalito Boulevard and Spencer Avenue. Stay left on Sausalito to Sacramento Way on the left, just past the brown-shingled beauty at #654. It's unsigned but look for concrete steps with an iron railing and descend to Sunshine Avenue. Jag left about 50 feet, then continue on Sacramento Way, which does have a sign here, on the right. These are more improved concrete steps with two railings, making it easier and safer to enjoy the views of the bay and the San Francisco–Oakland Bay Bridge. I write this on the day after the 7.1 earthquake which damaged part of the bridge and caused massive destruction in the Bay Area in October, 1989. These lanes, streets, and houses described here felt the 15-second tremor but, being built on solid bedrock, held up well.

Near the bottom of the path, views open to the hills to the west and the Waldo Tunnel and Grade of Route 101. Beyond, out of sight, are the Marin Headlands and the wide open 75,000 acres of the Golden Gate National Recreation Area. The pocket created by the curving hills is known locally as Hurricane Gulch for the strong winds that whip through and temperatures about 10 degrees colder than those where you're standing. This area, where you're walking now, is called the Banana Belt for its warmer climate.

Turn right, now on Central Avenue, continuing past North Street and past #41, where you'll see a stone alcove to the right as the street starts to bend. This is the start of the Cable Roadway, a footpath of steps on the left side (the steps on the right side of the alcove lead to a private residence). Soon dirt, grass, and concrete slabs replace the stone as the climb gets steeper, finishing with a solid wooden stairway up to Crescent Avenue. Go left, walking carefully on the left side of the small street, about 100 feet to Lower Crescent Avenue. A left drops you sharply to Oak Lane, a pathway that starts as steps with two iron rails just past #42. It continues with dirt and wood-plank steps down to more improved steps and views including Angel Island, the popular state park accessible by ferry from Tiburon.

Turn left on West Street, then straight to West Court, a cul-de-sac with improved steps at the end. Climb back up to Central, turn right and then find Sacramento Way, marked with a sign, next to a yellow and red fire hydrant, to the left. This brings you to Sunshine Avenue where you turn right. Where Sunshine veers right at a small stone wall, look to the left of the wall for a short set of steps and railing leading down to San Carlos Avenue.

Go left at the bottom, pass Cooper Lane, and retrace your steps as you carefully negotiate this street with no sidewalks. Usually it's better to walk on the left side of a street, facing traffic, but here the right side will be safer because of the curve of the street. As the spire of the captivating brown-shingled and stained-glass Christ Church comes into view, look for the Excelsior Path to the right just before the church. Descend the path, past Harrison, staying to the left of the old and intricate stone entrance way called "Nestledown." At the bottom, turn left on Bulkley, walking a few hundred feet to El Monte Lane, marked with a sign to the right. Savor views of the harbor and bay as you rendezvous at Bridgeway with the "wild Barbary Coast" shoppers and tourists of present-day Sausalito.

Sausalito: A Brief History

S ausalito has come a long way since 1775, when Spanish explorers on the first ship to pass through the Golden Gate named it Saucelitos, for the "little willows" that grew near a hillside spring. Whaling ships followed, drawn mainly by the fresh spring water, which allowed them to resupply and return to sea. By the mid-nineteenth century, a small community had developed to further serve the whalers. A ferry service to San Francisco followed in 1868, and the Northern Pacific Railroad made Sausalito its southern terminus a few years later.

It was a wild town in those days, "a haven for artists, writers and brothels," as one account put it. (Are artists and writers still put in the same category today?) The downtown area was a slice of Barbary Coast life with bordellos, saloons, and gambling dens, sanctioned by the city hall gang, and countered only by the crusades of the Sausalito Women's Club, which formed in 1913.

While the downtown was boiling and brewing, publisher William Randolph Hearst was building and living in a mansion enclave called "Sea Point" on a bluff overlooking the Garlic Belt, as the downtown was called; Jack London was reportedly writing his novel *Sea Wolf* at the old rooming house and saloon called "Castle-by-the-Sea"; and later, during Prohibition, mobster Baby Face Nelson was making a fortune smuggling bootleg whiskey into San Francisco from his headquarters at the "Silva Mansion" on Turney Street.

But the Golden Gate Bridge and World War II acted to settle the town somewhat. The bridge brought permanent residents who successfully lobbied for the rerouting of a proposed eight-lane highway through the center of town (the present Route 101 bypasses Sausalito, allowing it to preserve its small town atmosphere); and the war brought a shipyard with 20,000 workers building battleships 24 hours a day, seven days a week.

After the war a community of artists and literati rediscovered the town, and the ambience was like Paris's Left Bank. And when rents soared in·the sixties, many of these creative people moved to houseboats at Waldo Point to the north. But costs even there have risen, keeping bohemian residents to a minimum.

In 1976, the town was still going its own way, electing former madame, writer, and restaurateur Sally Stanford mayor as the national press looked on.

Today, the passenger ferry from the city brings thousands of visitors to this highly desirable tourists' Mecca. And as for present-day residents, Sausalito is the 45th wealthiest suburb in the United States. The place of little willows by the hillside spring has changed and will probably change again.

San Anselmo

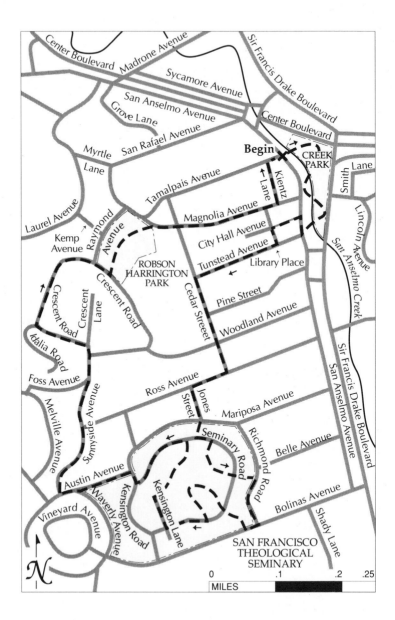

23

Creeks, Hills, & History

Terrain: *easy to moderate; improved lanes, bridges, and steps; unimproved paths*
Bus line: *20 (Golden Gate Transit)*
Parks: *Creek Park, Robson Harrington Park, Memorial Park, Sorich Ranch Park, Faude Park*
Shops: *San Anselmo Avenue, Sir Francis Drake Boulevard*
Distance: *3 miles*
Directions: *From 101 North, take Central San Rafael exit, turn left on Third Street and continue to the five-corner junction with Sir Francis Drake Boulevard. Turn left on Sir Francis Drake then take the first right to San Anselmo Avenue near the town hall.*

S an Anselmo, like most Marin towns, owes its existence and subsequent development to two events: the arrival of the narrow gauge Northern Pacific Coast Railroad in the late nineteenth century and the 1906 San Francisco earthquake, which made many former San Franciscan visitors to Marin permanent residents.

But San Anselmo, originally called Junction by the railroad, first got on the map because of one other event as well: the building of the San Francisco Theological Seminary, which opened in 1892 and whose beautiful grounds and original, castle-like, cut-stone buildings are featured in this walk.

San Anselmo Avenue is one of the oldest streets in town and

still is part of the hub of this community. San Anselmo Creek runs through the downtown area, with several footbridges connecting the street with a creekside park. Start on San Anselmo Avenue at Tamalpais Avenue, under a redwood entrance way marked "Creek Place" on the creek side of the street. Go under the entrance and its large posts and beams, turning right just before the bus stop. Enter a redwood grove, with picnic tables, into a small, quiet park next to the creek, a restful spot between two very busy streets: San Anselmo Avenue and Sir Francis Drake Boulevard. A wooden observation platform allows a good look at the year-round creek (there are steps leading down to the bank but that's about as far as they'll take you). Though tranquil most of the time, this creek has raged with three destructive floods in this century.

When you're ready to leave the park's lazy willows and lush lawn, continue to a bridge to the right, spanning the creek back to San Anselmo Avenue. Turn left and walk to a walkway, opposite Magnolia Avenue, again to the left, crossing another wooden bridge, with a small but active waterfall below. A right takes you along a sidewalk of Sir Francis Drake, and another right brings you to a more crafted walkway and bridge, of Japanese design, signed "On the Bridge." Benches and cool breezes here provide respite on hot days.

The bridge leads back to the main street, where the walkway comes out opposite the Spanish mission-style town hall, guarded by a lifelike stag on the front lawn. Cross San Anselmo at the Tunstead Avenue crosswalk to the left, then go just past the town hall, turning left on a path next to it which becomes City Hall Avenue. Turn left at Library Place, walking on the red brick sidewalk, past the library.

The next stretch is a series of town streets that are pleasant, quiet, and undistinguished, except for some attractive trees along the way, particularly elms, chosen as a street tree in much of San Anselmo and Ross for its impressive appearance and a root system that tends not to break up sidewalks and streets. The streets will take you to one of the showpieces of this walk, the San Francisco Theological Seminary, so go right on Tunstead, under the pines, left on Cedar Street, past Pine Street and Woodland Avenue, then a right on Ross Avenue (elms line the street), and a left onto short Jones Avenue, to where it joins Mariposa Avenue. As on the east coast, by the way, the elms have been plagued with Dutch elm disease, a fast-spreading affliction which forces the removal of affected trees from time to time. State forestry experts closely monitor these trees to keep the disease under control.

Now cross Mariposa, entering the grounds of the seminary (where visitors are entirely welcome and encouraged to explore the campus). Directly across the street, to the right of an asphalt driveway, is a small dirt path with a few stepping stones that winds in rough fashion, under a canopy of laurels, up to a wooden stairway, leading to Seminary Road. Turn left at the top, then right at the driveway behind the two oldest and most well known of the buildings on campus: Scott Hall, originally the library and now used for business offices, is the first you'll pass, and Montgomery Hall, initially used for student housing and now faculty offices and student services, is next to the right. These impressive medieval-like buildings were completed in 1892 with "Blue Stone" quarried in San Rafael and trim stone transported by horse and wagon from San Jose. There were 20 students when the seminary started then. Today there are 1,000. (The walk will bring you back to these buildings later.)

Continue on the driveway between the two buildings to the paths in front of Montgomery Hall. Take the path down toward the old oak tree, concrete bench, and stone wall. This particular California white oak is called the Bouick Oak, named after the seminary's first groundskeeper, Alexander Bouick, a man so beloved by the students that when he died in 1922, they named the tree in his honor, as well as donated the funds to build the wall, bench, and most of the paths going down the hill.

Descend the stone-lined steps to the left to Seminary Road. Cross and drop farther on a path, next to a small playground and surrounded by cypress, eucalyptus, and live oak, onto Richmond Road. Bear right to the Montgomery Chapel at the junction with Bolinas Avenue. This is the third-oldest building on campus, completed in 1897 and used originally for seminary services. It's still used for weddings and concerts and by various worship groups in the community. Notice the carvings above the entrance showing a human life span, from infancy to old age, and the name of the building's benefactor, Alexander Montgomery.

Walk around the building, admiring its Tiffany-inspired stained glass and its graceful palms standing sentry, to the adjacent driveway. Go up the wooden steps straight ahead, crossing the road to another path and steps immediately to the left. At the top, turn left, then left again onto a path marked by two wooden posts. Take a sharp left down a path and steps, walking quietly past faculty residences, to a red brick path leading back to Seminary Road. Walk to the right, past redwoods, ginkgoes, and pines, going right at the first street, Kensington Court. To the left, is the multiwindowed administration building, where you can pick up reference material about the seminary.

At the end of Kensington Court, go up a few steps, noticing the bell tower of Geneva Hall above and to the right. Seminary chimes ring on the hour, and hymns are played on the carillon of bells during services, concerts, and other special events. Continue to the right of Alexander Hall, up the steps, past toyon (also known as Christmasberry for its striking red berries against deep green foliage), madrone, olive, live oak, Monterey pine, cypress, and carob, a tree mentioned in the Bible. (In fact, there are about 20 tree species on campus that are mentioned in the Bible. An excellent guide, "Trees of San Francisco Theological

Seminary," is available at the bookstore in Alexander Hall.)

At the top of the hill is the whitewashed Geneva Hall to the left. Inside is an oil painting showing the seminary as it looked at the turn of the century. Continue down the steps ahead, walking in front of Scott Hall. The original tower was much taller and had clocks on each side, but it collapsed during the 1906 earthquake, crashing through the glass-domed library, through the assembly hall, and into the basement two floors below. Some of the original stones are still around you, lining the nearby paths and lawns.

Bear left onto Seminary Road, with views of Bald Hill (the Ross Valley's most prominent natural feature, currently in danger of commercial development, a prospect being countered by the "Save Bald Hill Committee," a group of San Anselmo and Ross residents) to the west, joining Kensington Road and Austin Avenue at the bottom. The bookstore is to your left in Alexander Hall. Leaving the Seminary grounds, take Austin, past Waverly Road and Sunnyside Avenue, going right at Melville Avenue. Bear right, past Vine Avenue, hiking up to Foss Avenue where you stay straight, with views of the Seminary, down to Sunnyside. Go left, past Woodland Avenue, to Crescent Road and bear left. Crescent passes Idalia Court, where deer sometime browse in front yards, then bends right, past the chaletlike house at #217, where just beyond is the entrance to Robson Harrington Park on the left.

The classic Victorian now houses offices, but the park's grounds and gardens are open to the public. Stay to the right and take the path next to the garden, with views of the surrounding ridges, down past the fig trees and playful klinker brick walls, bearing right near the bottom. Here a dirt path takes you past a brick, stone, and decorative tile picnic enclosure with an outdoor fireplace, ending under a brick archway. A right on tiny Magnolia Avenue leads out to Cedar Street. Cross and continue on Magnolia, past Library Place. A left on the backstreet, Kientz

Lane, takes you back to Tamalpais, with views of Red Hill to the north. (The soil composition is such on this hill that after a rain it turns a striking red.) A right on Tamalpais returns you to San Anselmo Avenue, where this journey into another century began.

Rain Walking

Word of rain coming rolls off the tongue so easily, without a trace of awe. We predict it, we bemoan it, we demean it, we try to pray it away, as if it were sent just to foil our weekend plans. And it is not until drought that we beat our chests, vowing never to vilify it again.

Walking in rain is like strolling with a good friend on a Sunday afternoon. Without resistance to its wetness, it touches in many ways — a bouquet of mist, a penetrating downpour, a slow, steady drizzle, a wild storm. Each rain is different, yet is somehow connected to all the rains that ever fell.

Reflection comes easier in the rain. The wetness directs thoughts inward. It's a good time to walk alone — slowly, without any direction. It's a good time for mulling, focusing on a problem rather than its solution.

Rain is a reminder to be still, to slow down, to sip a cup of tea, or to hold your lover's hand, stroke your child's head, allow your cat to sit undisturbed on your lap for a couple of hours. Clarity and peace come. Problems are not so big. Worry doesn't last.

The storm has passed, and a patch of pale blue sky appears. The inwardness rain cultivates helps prepare for the outwardness of the clearing. The sun gleams in the late afternoon. Damp streets reflect the gilded edges of things. Dark clouds drift east, still dense and serious. The rain has softened the landscape, has rounded its corners. Millions of clear droplets cling to all they touch. Lines of distinction disappear, revealing a crystalline embroidery that unifies the world. The light over the hills makes the mundane magical.

The rain has nourished the earth. Energies rise after the fall. It is a good time to be out walking. Smells from eucalyptus and live oak and redwood freshen and fill the senses while rejuvenating the mind. It is a good time for walking without

destination. The street is quieter and the songs of birds clearer.
It is a good time for breathing deeply and contemplating ordinary
things.

Fairfax

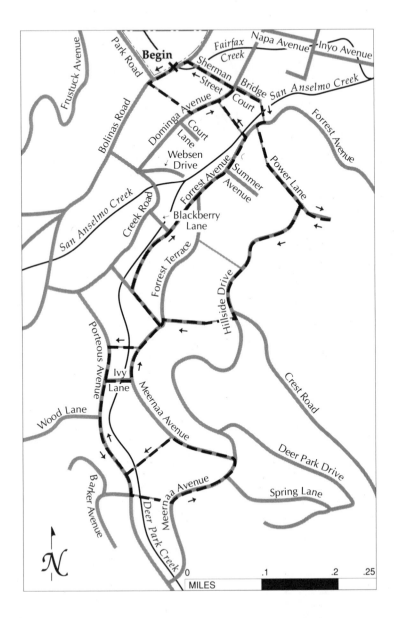

24
Up in the Valley

Terrain: *easy to steep; improved lanes, steps, and bridges; unimproved paths*

Special equipment: *shoes with good traction and/or a walking stick*

Bus lines: *20 to San Anselmo then transfer to 23 (Golden Gate Transit)*

Parks: *Deer Park*

Shops: *downtown Fairfax, San Anselmo, and San Rafael*

Distance: *2.2 miles*

Directions: *Route 101 to Sir Francis Drake Boulevard heading west. In San Anselmo, bear left at five corners intersection, staying on Sir Francis Drake. Continue to Fairfax. Left onto Bolinas Avenue from Main Street. Town hall is on right a few blocks down.*

The land of present-day Fairfax first belonged to a Mexican soldier, Don Domingo Sais, who was given 6,000 acres in 1839 as payment for military service. It was common practice for Spanish authorities considered California land next to worthless. He called his grant "Rancho Canada de Herrera," or Land of the Blacksmiths. But by 1853, hard-luck gold rushers had squatted on most of his land, driving Sais to suicide as his holdings became smaller and smaller.

Lord Charles Snowden Fairfax, another gold rush refugee, but a man of considerably more integrity than the squatters (he was a member of Virginia's founding family), bought land from the Sais family, settled, and became involved in local and state politics. After he died in 1869, the town was named in his honor and remained an agricultural area until the first subdivision for homes came in 1908. The Fairfax Incline Railway came soon after, bringing tourists and, during Prohibition, patrons to a bootleg tavern at the top of Manor Hill. Someone got the railroad condemned, however, and the whole operation shut down in 1929.

The town was the location for many early western movies and saw such silent screen stars as Tom Mix, Bronco Billy Anderson, Slim Summerville, and Hoot Gibson in the early twenties. It incorporated in 1931 with a population of 2,500. And in 60 years it has only increased by about 5,000. Don Domingo and Lord Charlie might feel cramped but there's still a lot of open space and quiet lanes as this walk will show.

On Bolinas Road, at the town hall and park, walk away from the center of town to Park Lane, cross Bolinas, and take the path, directly opposite Park. It's a small lane between a wood fence and cyclone fence, that shortcuts to Dominga Avenue. Go left on Dominga, past Sherman Avenue, walking right at Bridge Court, beyond Sherman. This looks like a private driveway, but at the end of this public right-of-way, to the right of the house there, is the start of a solid wooden bridge that spans San Anselmo Creek. The hidden bridge is heavily shaded, and is suspended high above the meandering year-round creek.

After the bridge, steps lead up to Forrest Avenue where you make a quick left then a right, just before #299, up a driveway/right-of-way to another asphalt right-of-way, before the street bends to the left. Another identifying marker is a telephone pole just before the right turn with a small sign marked #301. Again this looks private but is a public way that winds up to a sharp left on a dirt path before the house ahead. You can see the utility pipes half buried in this path as you walk up, past

#299, on wood plank and dirt steps, to Power Lane. This path may be difficult to negotiate after heavy rains.

Go left on the paved Power, climbing steeply to Hillside Avenue. Behind you are views of the town and a ridge above the valley known as Pam's Blue Ridge for a young woman who took her own life there.

At Hillside, take a short diversion to the left, past all the "Private Property" signs — the street is public — to see the house at the end and below. It had been abandoned for years, home to the same kind of squatters that drove Domingo Sais to his death, but was recently reclaimed and renovated. The Grecian Revival front of the house is reported to be an actual facade from the 1915 Panama Pacific International Exposition in San Francisco (which Maybeck helped design). And the pool in front is a replica of one at the exposition. A trail to the right of the cul-de-sac is one often used by students going to a high school in San Anselmo about half a mile away.

Now return, walking down Hillside, past Power, to expansive valley and ridge views as the street bends left. One of the few bothersome dogs on all of the walks in this book lives along here, but, at this writing, he seems to be all bark and no bite.

Continue to the junction with Crest Road and look for wooden steps and railing, on the right, next to a phone pole and fire hydrant. Take this sturdy stairway of 213 steps into the valley, past the hillside garden of the grounds called "Squirrel Hill." In the late forties, the town wanted to tear these steps out, fearing litigation if someone fell on them, but local residents raised their protesting voices and saved this heirloom.

At the bottom is Forrest Terrace, where you go left to Meernaa Avenue. Continue straight on Meernaa to a dirt and grass shortcut, just past #48, on the right. Walk through to Porteous Avenue, turn left, walking past Ivy Lane and Wood Lane, to a path on the left opposite Barker Avenue. If you continue straight on Porteous, you'll enter Deer Park Meadows, a great hiking and picnicking area.

The path starts as dirt next to a phone pole, goes under boughs of spruce and pine, and quickly crosses little Deer Park Creek via a wood footbridge. The path leads out to Meernaa where you go left, past "The Tree House" at #161, under the old live oaks, past Spring Lane, as the street bends to the left, and then continuing left on Meernaa where Hillside goes straight. There's a small First Bay Tradition home at #132, then, just past #108, see a path on the left and a sign, "Foot Path Only." Enter past fig trees, Christmasberries, laurels, cedars, and a chicken coop with its clucking flock, out and over another small wooden bridge to Porteous.

Go right to another right on Ivy Lane, then a left on Meernaa, noting the whimsical fence and color TV/Mickey Mouse lawn decoration at #51. Continue on Meernaa, bearing left, past a row of olive trees, the olives of which look tempting but must be specially treated before being edible. At Forrest, bear right, up past Blackberry Lane, past a few of the quaint, shingled cottages Fairfax has many of, past Forrest Terrace and Summer Avenue to a driveway/right-of-way on the left, marked by the numbers 306, 302, 298, and 294. Descend the concrete driveway to a path directly between the two houses below, specifically to the left of #298. There's a large arborvitae shrub hiding the path, which leads to a wooden bridge traversing San Anselmo Creek.

It's a safe bridge, but I wouldn't do the boogaloo (does anyone still do the boogaloo?) across it. Instead, consider stopping awhile and absorbing the sounds and smells of this riparian environment.

Across the bridge, a walkway leads out to Dominga, where you cross to Sherman and then out to the main street, Bolinas. Across the street, you can finish this walk by exploring the small city park, with its cool redwood grove, paths around the town hall, benches, a contained San Anselmo Creek, and the Pavilion —

the old community hall further back, built in 1921 on an Indian mound. The building became a lively dance hall during the "Big Band" era and was renamed "The Coconut Grove" at that time. It's still used occasionally for events, but its heyday has passed.

In the late 1800s, this part of town was the terminus for a railroad from the Tiburon Peninsula, and, as one account puts it, "was used as a park and meeting place and the scene of countless brawls." For once, it's a quieter place than it used to be.

"The California Garden"

A s to the precise form which this new garden type of California should assume, it is perhaps premature to say, but
but one thing is vital, that at least a portion of the space should
be sequestered from public view, forming a room walled in with
growing things and yet giving free access to light and air. To
accomplish this there must be hedges or vine-covered walls or
trellises, with rustic benches and tables to make the garden
habitable. If two or more of these bowers are planned, connected
by sheltered paths, a center of interest for the development of
the garden scheme will be at once available. My own preference
for a garden for the simple home is a compromise between the
natural and formal types—a compromise in which the carefully
studied plan is concealed by a touch of careless grace that makes
it appear as if nature had unconsciously made bowers and paths
and sheltering hedges.

In the selection of plants there is one point which may be
well kept in mind—to strive for a mass of bloom at all periods
of the year. . . .

Let us, then, by all means, make the most of our gardens, studying them as an art—the extensions of architecture into the
domain of life and light. Let us have gardens wherein we can
assemble for play or where we may sit in seclusion at work;
gardens that will exhilarate our souls by the harmony and glory
of pure and brilliant color, that will nourish our fancy with sug-
gestions of romance as we sit in the shadow of the palm and
listen to the whisper of rustling bamboo; gardens that will bring
nature to our homes and chasten our lives by contact with the
purity of the great Earth Mother.

Charles Keeler, from *The Simple Home,* 1904

Belvedere

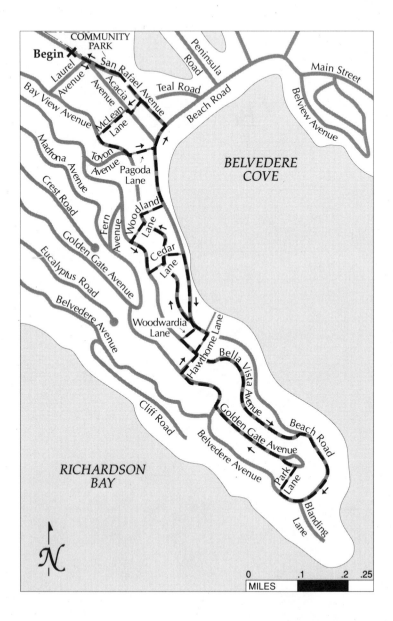

25
Belvedere Means "Beautiful View"

Terrain: *easy to steep; improved steps and lanes; unimproved paths*
Bus line: *10*
Parks: *Community Park*
Shops: *downtown Tiburon, Boardwalk Shopping Center*
Distance: *3.1 miles*
Directions: *From 101, take Tiburon exit, heading towards Tiburon. Turn right at San Rafael Avenue and follow to city hall opposite Laurel Avenue. The next street is Community Road, where there is parking at the rear of city hall.*

Before Belvedere became the yachting capital of the Pacific Coast, before it became one of the most exclusive residential areas in America, it was just another place to graze cows. That was in the mid-nineteenth century. And it wasn't until late in that century that wealthy San Franciscans saw the advantages of this fabulous peninsula. One man, though, named Israel Kashow, saw it much earlier, settling there with his wife in 1855 and raising five children.

The only vestige of Kashow that remains though, is an old pear tree, marked by a commemorative sign, in front of Community Park, next to the town hall. Kashow was ignominiously evicted from the land in 1885 by the heirs to John Reed, the early settler who grazed cattle there and built the mill that led to the founding of Mill Valley. What developers subsequently planned and built is a storybook town with magnificent Victorians, winding streets, hidden lanes and steps, all neatly marked with signs decorated with paintings of harbor scenes, and, almost everywhere, some of the finest views in the Bay Area.

This walk begins at the town hall/Community Park area on San Rafael Avenue. Walk on San Rafael toward the bay and look for McLean Lane, marked on the right with an artistic sign on a white post. Go up the path and steps, with iron rail, past little Acacia Avenue, continuing on older concrete steps up to Bay View Avenue. Turn left up to Pagoda Lane, next to a brown-shingled garage on the left, neatly marked as are all the lanes in this town that obviously cherishes its pathways. Descend the concrete steps with wooden railing to views of the Bay Bridge and the harbor. Along with the views there are also shingled cottages, live oaks, wild gardens, and old stone-lined steps near the bottom.

The steps become an asphalt path winding down to Beach Road, where you go right, past the San Francisco Yacht Club and a row of graceful palms lining the road. That's Angel Island you're looking at in the bay. Very shortly, notice Woodland Lane on the right, next to #157, and scale the stone and concrete steps to Bay View. Jag left then continue up Woodland on the right. Just look for the painted sign. This brings you to Bella Vista Avenue, another street name that celebrates the views.

Go left, carefully, on this narrow street, to Cedar Lane, which is a bit tricky to find since the sign is facing in the other direction. The path is next to #270, and you'll need to take a sharp left onto an unimproved lane with a wood railing. It's directly across from the end of an attractive stone wall. The path turns to the right, and the condition of it improves as it becomes steps. The great old Victorian to the left is a prime example of the mansions that were built near the turn of the century when Belvedere developed and grew. There's a huge live oak at the bottom that grew and developed even before the Victorian, as the steps merge with Bay View.

Turn left and find the continuation of Cedar Lane about 50 feet to the right, just before #266. Descend sharply, holding onto the rail as you view the expansive view. At the bottom is Beach again, where you go right, past gliding brown pelicans and sailboats, and the public access iron steps that lead down to the shore. If you don't mind the walk back up, the small sandy area at the bottom might be a good spot to read, picnic, soak your feet, or launch a raft.

Continue on Beach as it narrows — making the walking somewhat precarious — and joins Bay View. Stay straight, past #246 and its great shingled roof, to Woodwardia Lane on the right, opposite #270. The old path and steps lift you charmingly to Bella Vista, where a left soon brings you back to Beach. The road here bends to the right, and a lookout with wood rail and concrete bench allows views of a part of the bay known as Raccoon Straits.

The street now becomes Belvedere Avenue, continuing past Blanding Lane to the wooden stairway called Park Lane on the right, opposite #443. The path above the stairs is rougher than most in town but pleasantly passable as it takes you to Golden Gate Avenue, a cul-de-sac. Go left, but before you leave the circle, see the inspiring views of the Golden Gate Bridge and the Marin Headlands to the southwest. The bridge brought much growth to Belvedere as it did to all Marin towns after it was completed in 1937.

Head west out of the cul-de-sac, past Pine Avenue toward the brown-shingled First Bay Tradition house and around the bend to the Hawthorne Lane, with its sign on a garage, partially obscured by shrubs, next to #304. Take these steps down to Bella Vista, turn left and find the continuation of the lane to the right. This brings you to Bay View, where you turn left and walk down Woodland Lane to the right, just past #242. This steep descent ends at Beach Road by the yacht club and palm trees. Go left and cross at the walk in front of the club; go left again, then bear right as the street becomes San Rafael Avenue, which leads you back to the town hall and Community Park and the pear tree of Israel Kashow. He must have been a sad man, indeed, when they evicted him from this place of beautiful views.

Walking & Watching

Walking for walking's sake is full of wonders — wonders that surface when walking loses its purpose. When the walking is to get somewhere or do something or for something, the focus is on the result: food at the market, money at the bank, a chocolate treat, the Sunday paper. The walking itself is easily ignored — the joys of contacting the earth, of moving along in the present moment, of watching and listening.

Can walking be not only for exercise, or as a venue for talking to a friend, or getting to a business appointment, but for walking itself? The union of ground and feet — sometimes hard and unyielding, sometimes soft and springy, rocky and sharp, silky and lush, muddy and cool, or baked and hot. The withered winter flower, the young velvety grass on a distant hillside after the first heavy rains, the endless trek of ants lugging nesting material back to their hill in the summer, the fragrant chamomile, the cool light before the sun has risen and after it sets.

No one will measure success by these things. There will be no tangible reward for smelling a flower or stopping to see the tops of trees sway in the breeze. They may not build a better body or cure depression. But what does happen with simple and innocent observation is heightened sensitivity. And with sensitivity, thoughts and actions are less self-centered. There is more appreciation of and connection to Earth and its inhabitants. And with that bond come compassion and love. Walking for the sake of walking, watching for the sake of watching, can help the planet heal simply by not harming it.

Then, you might stop and take an injured bird to a wildlife rescue center. Then, you may find a home for a kitten that someone has thrown into the woods. Then, perhaps you will remove a branch that has fallen on the path so the next walker can continue unimpeded. Then, you will more likely leave a flower unpicked for others to enjoy, or remove a piece of litter

and dignify not only the path but the entire community.

It is walking with awareness and care. It is leaving the path a better place than before, not out of obligation but response-ability. It is walking as a creative act, enhancing your life, all life.

Supplemental Reading

The Berkeley Architectural Heritage Association. *Walking Tours of Berkeley, California.* (A pamphlet periodically revised.)

Freudenheim, Leslie Mandelson, and Sussman, Elisabeth Sachs. *Building with Nature: Roots of the San Francisco Bay Region Tradition.* Santa Barbara: Peregrine Smith, Inc., 1974.

Keeler, Charles. *The Simple Home.* San Francisco: P. Elder, 1904.

McArdle, Phil, ed. *Exactly Opposite the Golden Gate.* Berkeley: Heyday Books, 1989.

Margolin, Malcolm, and Pitcher, Don. *Berkeley Inside/Out.* Berkeley: Heyday Books, 1989.

Pettitt, George A. Berkeley. *The Town and Gown of It.* Berkeley: Howell-North Books, 1973.

Wilson, Mark A. *East Bay Heritage: A Potpourri of Living History.* San Francisco, California Living Books, 1979.

A wealth of material on the towns and walks mentioned in this guide can be found in the Mill Valley Public Library History Room, the Oakland Public Library History Room, the Piedmont Community Hall History Room, the Anne Kent California Room of the Marin Civic Center Public Library, and the Bancroft Library at UC Berkeley.

(PHOTO BY GLORIA ST. JOHN)

About the Author

When asked what he does for a living, Stephen Altschuler replied, "I walk, and sometimes write about where I walk and what I think about when I walk, and, at times, get paid for this. At least that's the plan." He has been a freelance writer/photographer since 1970, having published numerous articles in local, regional, and national publications, including *East West Journal; Yankee; Writer's Digest; The Humanist; San Francisco Chronicle; Los Angeles Times; Boston Globe; Maine Times;* and *The Walking Magazine.* As is the case with many writers, he has had a wide variety of other jobs such as prison social worker, cross-country skiing instructor, golf pro, music therapist and performer, marriage and family counselor, college academic advisor, radio show producer, and woodsman. His New Hampshire–based radio program, *Backwoods Cabin,* was a weekly journal of a city-bred man's experiences living in a primitive backwoods cabin, which he dwelled in for four years.

He was born in Philadelphia, lived in New England for a number of years, and has called the Bay Area his home since 1982. At some point, while his legs are still strong and his spirit willing, he plans to walk around the world in search of more hidden pathways both inner and outer. This is his first book.